Hacking for Beginners

Mastery Guide to Learn and Practice the Basics of Computer and Cyber-security

Richard Dorsel

Respective authors own all copyrights not held by the publisher.

The information herein is offered for informational purposes solely, and is universal as so. The presentation of the information is without contract or any type of guarantee assurance.
The trademarks that are used are without any consent, and the publication of the trademark is without permission or backing by the trademark owner. All trademarks and brands within this book are for clarifying purposes only and are the owned by the owners themselves, not affiliated with this document

Table of Contents

INTRODUCTION

In The first years of cyber-attacks, associations would wait to get assaulted until they developed a more thorough plan and reaction to the attacker. The attack could leave the associations' network presence down and useless for days. Several reasons cyber-attacks could impair a network at early days with the malicious behavior are perhaps not enough focused research on protecting and preventing and also the absence of a coordinated campaign between private industry and the federal government.

Since The very first popular and endemic cyber-attack from the mid-1990's, most professionals in private and public associations have been analyzing and taking care of the issue of cyber-attacks. Initially security businesses such as Norton, McAfee, Trend Micro, etc., approached the situation in the reactive position. They knew hackers/malicious attackers were likely to strike. The objective of what's currently called Intrusion Detection Systems (IDS) would be to find a malicious attacker before the anti-virus, Trojan horse, or pig was used to attack. When the attacker has been able to attack on the system, security professionals could dissect this code. Once the code has been dissected, a reply or "fix" has been implemented to the infected system (s). The "fix" is currently known as a touch and they're always downloaded across the system as per week upgrades to prevent known attacks. Even though IDS is still a wait and see position, security professionals are becoming a great deal more complicated in their approach and it continues to evolve as a portion of their arsenal.

Security Professionals started studying the situation out of a preventative angle. This transferred the cybersecurity industry from defensive to offensive manner. They're troubleshooting how to protect against an attack on an individual network or system. In accordance with this type of thinking, an Intrusion Prevention Systems (IPS) called Snort (2010) was soon introduced. Snort is just a mix IDS and IPS open-source applications available at no cost download. Employing IDS/IPS pc software such as Snort allows security professionals to be more proactive in the cyber-security arena. Though IPS allows security professionals to engage in crime in addition to defense, they usually do not rest on the laurels nor do they even prevent tracking the utilization of malicious attackers that cultivated imagination, imagination, and invention. Additionally, it enables security professionals who shield the cyber-world to remain equal or a single step in front of attackers.

Cybersecurity Additionally has an offensive and defensive part in the market. In its cyber-security commercial, The University of Maryland University College (2012) says that there will likely soon be"fifty thousand occupations out there in cybersecurity during the subsequent ten decades." The faculty was conducting this commercial for at least a couple of decades. After the industrial first began running they offered thirty thousand jobs. They've demonstrably corrected the forecast higher depending upon studies in addition to the private and government industry pinpointing cyber-security as a crucial requirement to shield critical infrastructure.

Cybersecurity Can play economical defense by protecting those tasks which handle domestic security concerns and has to stay the in the USA. Even the cybersecurity sector is driven by federal security from the government kingdom and intellectual property (IP) from the private sector. Most U.S. organizations whine about the government about foreign states hijacking their applications suggestions and creations through state regulated and coordinated crime hackers. Given that foreign nations condone country sponsored domestic security and intellectual property strikes, it is on the power of organizations to come across human funding over the shores of America to successfully execute the duties and activities needed.

On The offensive side, cyber-security can induce growth and boost the skill sets of residents in cities such as Prince George's County, Maryland which sits at the epicenter of cybersecurity for its state of Maryland and the world. Prince George's Community College is your house of Cyberwatch and the principal hub for cybersecurity training and most effective techniques that has pushed out into different community colleges which are a part of their consortium. The objective of those community colleges would be to emphasise with the instruction offered to students using skills that employers say are required to function as "work force prepared" It's likewise a rich recruiting ground for technology organizations throughout the united states to determine and hire human-capital to placed up front lines of their U.S. struggle in cyber-security. Since Maryland Senator Barbara Mikulski (2012) says the students are willing to function as"cyberwarriors" and inturn function ready.

Cyber-security Is the security of internet-connected processes, including hardware, applications and data, from cyber-attacks. In a computing context, security comprises cyber-security and physical security are both used by businesses to safeguard against unauthorized usage of data centers and other unmanned systems. The objective of cyber-security would be to limit risk and protect IT resources from attackers with malicious purpose. Information security, that was made to keep the confidentiality, integrity and accessibility of data, can be really a sub set of all cyber-security.

Cyber-security Best techniques can, and should, be executed by large and tiny associations, individuals and employees. Probably one of the most problematic elements of cyber-security is that the always evolving nature of security risks and complex persistent dangers (APTs).

The Classic approach is to target resources on key system components and also force away the biggest understood dangers, which meant departing components un-defended and perhaps not protecting systems against dangerous threats. To take care of the present ecosystem, advisory associations are encouraging a more proactive and more flexible strategy.

The National Institute of Standards and Technology (NIST)," as an instance, recently issued updated tips in its own hazard assessment framework that urge a shift toward continuous observation and real-time evaluations. Version 1.1 of this Length for Enhancing Critical Infrastructure premiered in April 2018. The voluntary cyber-security Framework (CSF), developed for usage from the banking, communications, security and energy businesses, maybe embraced by most industries, including state and federal authorities. President Donald-Trump issued an executive order mandating that federal agencies embrace the NIST CSF in might 20 17.

What is Cyber-security

Cyber-security Is a defensive remedy to guard virtually any internet-connected system out of cyber-threats and strikes.

Purpose Of all cyber-security

Cyber-security Measures should be executed to guard the data of little and huge associations as well as individuals. Though significant security breaches would be the people which frequently get treated, little companies still need to bother themselves using their own security position, since they could usually be the mark of malware and viruses.

Exactly why Is cyber-security crucial?

Cyber-security Is very vital since it may help protect the organization's data resources out of digital strikes which may damage the company or individuals when placed at the incorrect hands. Medical, corporate, government and economic records hold private info. Security events may result in losses concerning standing, money and theft of data, deletion of information and fraud.

What Cyber-security can protect against

Cyber-security Helps prevent information breaches, identity theft and ransom-ware strikes, in addition to helping in hazard management. As soon as a business has a powerful awareness of network security and also an effective incident response program, it really is best able to mitigate and prevent cyber-attacks. The procedure for staying intouch with innovative technologies, security trends and hazard intellect is a trying undertaking.

Types Of all cyber-security risks

Cyber-threats Can take several shapes, including these:

Malware: a sort of malicious applications by which any document or application is utilized to harm your personal computer user, like worms, computer viruses, and Trojan horses and spyware.

Ransom-ware: a kind of malware which involves a individual locking the casualty's computer files normally via encryption and also requiring a payment to authenticate and unlock them.

Social technology: an attack which centers upon individual interaction to deceive users to dividing security procedures to get sensitive information that's typically protected.

Phishing: a sort of fraud where faked mails are shipped which resemble mails from respectable sources nonetheless, the purpose of these mails would be to steal sensitive data, such as bank card or login details.

Cyber-security Hazard vectors

A Hazard vector is really a course or way where a hacker could access a laptop or system host to deliver a payload or malicious effect. Strike vectors let hackers to exploit system vulnerabilities, including individual operators. Popular assault vectors comprise these:

USB-Sticks and other mobile storage apparatus

- unsupported browser extensions
- infected sites
- orphan accounts
- advertisement
- online quizzes and personality tests

Elements Of all cyber-security

Additionally, it Can be quite challenging in cyber-security to stay informed about the shifting security risks. The standard approach is to focus funds on key platform components. Now, ensuring cyber-security demands the coordination of efforts through the duration of a data platform, which comprises these:

- Software safety: Reduce the probability that unauthorized code should be in a position to govern software to get, steal, alter or delete sensitive data.
- Data security (infosec): Shield information resources, no matter how the data is structured or whether it's in transit, has been processed or are in rest in storage.
- Network-security: Detect, prevent and react to risks with using security policies, applications tools plus it services.
- Business continuity planning (BCP)/disaster recovery preparation (DRP): Keep or fast restart mission-critical functions after a tragedy.
- Operational security (opsec): Classify information resources, and also determine the controllers needed to safeguard these resources.
- Enduser instruction: Supply directives that clarify what activities employees must choose or avoid so that you can secure corporate resources.

One Among the very problematic components of cyber-security is that the always evolving nature of security risks. As new technologies emerge and current technologies is employed in fresh or unique ways, fresh paths of attack have been manufactured also. Maintaining with all these continual modifications and progress in strikes and upgrading methods to protect them against them could be hard for associations. Additionally, this includes making certain every one of the elements of cyber-security are always changed and upgraded to protect against potential vulnerabilities. This could be particularly hard for smaller businesses.

In Addition, Now, there's a whole lot of possible data a business could gather on those who get involved in another of the own services. Using an increase of data being accumulated, the odds of a cyber-criminal who would like to sneak PII is just another concern. By way of instance, a business which stores PII from the cloud could possibly be at the mercy of a ransomware attack and really should do exactly what it is to protect against a cloud violation.

Cyber-security Should additionally address cloud-based instruction, as employees can accidentally attract a virus into an office in their job computer, notebook or smartphone.

Still another Large challenge to cyber-security could be your staffing shortage. As growth data in organizations becomes increasingly important, the demand for more cyber-security personnel with the best necessary abilities to investigate, manage and respond to events rises. It's projected there are just two million un-filled cyber-security projects worldwide. Cyber-security Ventures also estimated that, by 2021, you will see up to 3.5 million un-filled cyber-security projects.

Automation

New Advances in machine learning and artificial intelligence (AI) are increasingly being developed which help security professionals organize and manage log data. AI and machine learning can help in areas having data driven data streams, like these:

- correlating data by coordinating it, pinpointing potential dangers and calling an attacker's following measure;
- discovering infections by implementing a security system which could analyze data and comprehend dangers;
- generating protections without putting a strain on tools; along with

- always auditing the efficacy of protections set up to guarantee they're working.

Cyber-security vendors

As a consequence of rising security threats, investments in cyber-security services and technologies are climbing. Gartner forecast that global spending on information security services and products and services could hit $114 billion in 2018 and a second 8.7% rise to $124 billion in 20-19.

Vendors In cyber-security areas will on average utilize endpoint, network and complex hazard protection safety, in addition to data loss avoidance (DLP). Three well-known cyber-security vendors are Cisco, McAfee and Trend Micro.

Cisco Has a tendency to concentrate on networks and empowers its clients to work with firewalls, virtual private networks (VPNs) and advanced level antivirus security, together with encouraging email and end point security. Cisco also supports real-time malware blocking.

McAfee Makes cyber-security services and products for consumers and enterprise clients. McAfee supports cellular telephone, enterprise clouds, network, web and Server based security. Data security and security will be also offered.

Trend Micro is a antimalware seller that features threat coverage for mobile, hybrid vehicle clouds, SaaS and the net of things (IoT). Trend Micro provides users with end-point, email and security.

Careers In cyber-security

That the cyberthreat landscape keeps growing and new dangers emerge -- including as dangers in the landscape of IoT -- humans are essential with awareness and skills of the security hardware and applications.

IT Professionals and different household specialists are wanted in security tasks, like these:

Chief information security officer (CISO): This person implements the security application across the company and manages the IT security department's operations.
Security engineer: This Person protects business assets from dangers having a focus on quality management over the IT infrastructure.

Safety builder: they is in charge of planning, assessing, designing, analyzing, maintaining and encouraging a business's critical infrastructure.

Safety analyst: This individual has a lot of responsibilities which have preparation security controls and measures and protecting digital files, and ranning both external and internal security audits.

History

Crucial Milestones in cyber-security history include these:

- Back in 1971, the creeper virus has been found; nevertheless, it really is often called the first virus.
- At 1983, Massachusetts Institute of Technology (MIT) has been awarded a patent for a cryptographic communications strategy and procedure -- that the very first cyber-security patent.
- From the 1990s, the arrival of computer viruses resulted in the disease of tens of thousands of personal computers (PCs), inducing cyber-security to develop into household dilemma and easing the production of antivirus program.
- Back in 1993, the initial DEFCON seminar occured; its own attention was cyber-security.

- Back in 2003, Anonymous has been formed -- the very first renowned cookie group.

- In 2013, the Goal breach happened by which 40 million debit and credit card records were obtained and discharged.

- In 20-16, Yahoo reported two cyber-security breaches in that hackers gained access to data out of over 500 million user account.

- In 2017, the Equifax security violation happened, which exposed the personal information up to 147 million people.

- In 2018, the General Data protection Legislation (GDPR) has been executed. It dedicated to the security of end user data from the European Union (EU).

- Additionally in 2018, the California Consumer Privacy Act (CCPA) has been executed. It encourages individuals' right to restrain their particular PII.

- In Conclusion, cyber-security has come a ways as the more publicized hacking cases of the 1990's (Krebs, 2003). These events attracted awareness of the demand for its very best and brightest to get into the area of network and computer security with the role of inventing strategies and methods to shield against "bad actors" which could utilize technology to perpetrate malicious acts. Due network and computer security require STEM (Science, Technology, Engineering, q) skills, the swimming of U.S. born applicants is currently tiny. This introduces an economic development opportunity for locales using their public colleges since technology training reasons which are closely intertwined with tech organizations who want the individual funding. The overarching objective of the stakeholders would be always to produce "workforce ready" students.

CHAPTER ONE
WHAT IS CYBER-SECURITY?

Additionally Called information security, cyber-security denotes the custom of ensuring that the integrity, integrity, and accessibility (ICA) of advice. Cyber-security is included of an evolving collection of tools, hazard management procedures, engineering, training, and recommendations designed to safeguard devices, networks, programs, and also data in strikes or unauthorized access.

Exactly why Is cyber-security crucial?

The World is based on technology greater than ever. Because of this, digital data production has soared. Now, organizations and authorities save an excellent deal of the data on computers and also transmit it around networks into additional computers. Devices and their inherent systems have vulnerabilities which, when tapped, sabotage medical insurance and objectives of a company.

A Data breach could have a variety of catastrophic consequences for almost any business enterprise. It can interrupt a organization's standing through the increased loss of partner and consumer confidence. The increasing loss of crucial information, such as source files or intellectual property, may cost a company its competitive gain. Moving farther, a data breach may impact corporate earnings as a result of noncompliance with data security regulations. It's estimated that, normally, a statistics breach costs an influenced organization $3.6 million. With high profile statistics breaches making media reports, it's crucial that businesses embrace and execute a powerful cyber-security strategy.

Common Different types of cyber-security

Network Security protects traffic by controlling incoming and outgoing links to stop dangers from spreading or entering on the system.

Data Decline Prevention (DLP) protects data by simply emphasizing the place, classification and observation of information in the rest, being used and also in motion.

Cloud Security provides security for data used in cloud-based applications and services.

Intrusion Detection Systems (IDS) or Intrusion Prevention Systems (IPS) work to spot potentially hostile cyber actions.

Identity And Access Management (IAM) utilize authentication solutions to confine and track employee usage of protect internal systems from malicious issues.

Encryption Is the practice of communicating data to render it sporadically, and it is frequently used during data transport to stop theft.

Antivirus/anti-malware Solutions scanning pcs for known threats. Present day solutions are able to find previously unknown dangers based in their behavior.

Cyber-security is also the practice of shielding systems, Networks, and apps out of digital strikes. All these cyber-attacks usually are geared toward obtaining, changing, or even ruining sensitive advice; extorting money from users; or interrupting normal business procedures.

Implementing powerful Cyber-security steps is Especially difficult today since there are more apparatus than humans, and they're getting to be more sophisticated.

What's cyber-security about?

A Successful cyber-security system has multiple layers of security spread over the servers, programs, networks, or data this you plans to stay safe. In a business, many individuals, procedures, and technology needs to all complement each other to generate an effective shield against cyberattacks. Even a unified hazard management system may automate integrations across select Cisco Security services and products and quicken key security surgeries works: detection, analytics, and remediation.

People

Users Must know and comply with all basic data security fundamentals such as choosing passwords that are strong being wary of attachments from email, and also burning data. Learn more regarding basic cyber-security fundamentals.

Procedures

Businesses Musthave a frame for the way they handle both successful and attempted cyberattacks. 1 well-respected framework can direct you. It explains ways to identify strikes, protect procedures, find and react to risks, and get over attacks that are successful. See a movie description of this NIST Cyber-security frame.

Technology

Tech Is critical to giving individuals and organizations that the computer system security tools required to safeguard themselves from cyberattacks. Three chief things have to be shielded: end point apparatus such as computers, smart mobile devices, and routers; computers; and also the cloud. Common technology used to guard those things incorporate next-generation firewalls, DNS filtering malware security, anti-virus applications, and email security solutions.

Exactly why is cyber-security crucial?

In Now's connected environment, everyone else advantages of complex cyberdefense programs. In an individual level, a cyber-security attack could lead to everything from identity theft, into extortion efforts, to the lack of significant data such as family photos. Everybody else depends upon infrastructures such as power plants, hospitals, and financial service businesses. Preventing these as well as other associations is important to keeping our society working out.

They show new vulnerabilities, educate the general public on the value of cyber-security, and fortify open-source tools. Their job may make the Internet easier for everybody.

Cyber-security is still the practice of protecting computers, Servers, cellular phones, electronic networks, systems, and data in malicious attacks. Additionally, it is called information tech security or electronic information security. The word applies in various contexts, in the business to traveling with a laptop, and will be broken to some common types.

- Network-security could be the custom of procuring a computer system from intrusion, whether targeted networked or opportunistic malware.

- Software safety centers around keeping applications and apparatus free of dangers. A compromised application can offer access to this data its own supposed to protect. Powerful security begins in the design period, well in front of a program or apparatus is set up.

- Data security protects the privacy and integrity of data, both in storage and in transit.

- Operational security contains the procedures and decisions for both protecting and handling data resources. Even the permissions users have when obtaining a system and also the processes which determine where and how data could be shared or stored fall under this umbrella.

- Disaster recovery and business continuity specify the way a business reacts to a cyber-security episode or some other event which results in the lack of data or operations. Disaster restoration policies dictate the method by which the corporation restores its surgeries and advice to go back to exactly the exact same operating capacity prior to the occasion. Business continuity is your master plan that the company falls straight back while attempting to use minus resources that are certain.

- Enduser education handles the very unpredictable cyber-security variable: people. Anybody can unwittingly introduce a virus into a otherwise immune system by neglecting to follow decent security practices. Invite users to delete questionable email attachments, maybe not plug-in anonymous USB drives, and also many other significant lessons is essential for the security of almost any company.

The grade of this cyber hazard

The U.S. government spends $1 9 billion annually [1] on Cyber-security but cautions that cyberattacks continue to grow at a rapid pace. To combat the development of malicious code and also help with early detection, the National Institute of Standards and Technology (NIST) recommends continuous, real-time observation of most electronic tools.

The dangers countered by Cyber-security are Three Fold:

Inch. Cyber-crime Comprises unmarried celebrities or bands targeting systems for profit or to result in disturbance.

2. Cyber-attack frequently entails politically motivated Information collecting.

3. Cyberterror is Meant to undermine digital systems To cause anxiety or fear.

Frequent methods attackers utilize to restrain computers Networks include viruses, viruses, spyware, viruses, Trojans, and ransom-ware. Viruses and worms may self-replicate and damage systems or files, whilst spyware and Trojans tend to be used for data collection that was overburdened. Ransom-ware waits for a chance to encrypt each of the consumer's information and requires payment to get usage of this consumer. Malicious code frequently spreads via an unsolicited email attachment or perhaps a legitimate-looking download which in fact conveys a malware payload.

Cyber-security risks affect all businesses, no matter size. The businesses that reported that the many cyber-attacks lately years have been healthcare, manufacturing, finance, and administration [2]. Several of those businesses are more attracting cyber-criminals because they amass financial and healthcare data, but most of organizations which use networks might be targeted to get customer data, corporate espionage, or even customer strikes.

End-user security

Therefore, just how can Cyber-security steps shield consumers and systems? To begin with, cyber-security is based on cryptographic protocols to encrypt mails, files, along with other data that is critical. This not only protects information from transit, but additionally protects against theft or loss. Moreover, end user security applications scans computers for bits of code that is malicious, quarantines this particular code, after which removes it from this system. Security apps may also find and remove malicious code concealed Master Boot Record (MBR) and built to reestablish or wipe data in your computer's hard disk drive.

Electronic safety protocols additionally Concentrate on real-time malware Detection. Many utilize heuristic and behavioral analytics to track the behavior of an app and its own code to shield against viruses or Trojans that change their shape with each implementation (polymorphic and metamorphic malware). Security programs can restrict possibly malicious software to a digital bubble different in the user's system to test their behavior and also learn to better find new ailments.

Security applications are still evolving new defenses as Cyber-security professionals identify new dangers and new tactics to combat them.

Intent Behind Cyber-security

Cyber-security Measures should be executed to guard the data of little and huge associations as well as individuals. Though significant security breaches would be the people which frequently get treated, little companies still need to bother themselves using their own security position, since they could usually be the mark of malware and viruses.

Exactly why is cyber-security crucial?

Cyber-security Is very vital since it may help protect a company's data resources from digital strikes which may damage the company or individuals when placed at the incorrect hands. Medical, corporate, government and economic records hold private info. Security events may cause losses concerning standing, money and theft of data, deletion of information and fraud.

Exactly what Cyber-security can Avoid

Cyber-security Helps prevent information breaches, identity theft and ransom-ware strikes, in addition to helping in hazard management. As soon as a business has a powerful awareness of network security and also an effective incident response program, it really is best able to mitigate and prevent cyber-attacks. The procedure for staying intouch with innovative technologies, security trends and hazard intellect is a trying undertaking.

Kinds of Cyber-security risks

Cyber-threats Can take several shapes, including these:

Malware: a sort of malicious applications by which any document or application may be utilized to harm your personal computer user, like viruses, viruses, computer viruses, and Trojan horses and spyware.

Ransom-ware: a kind of malware which calls for an individual locking the casualty's computer files normally via encryption and also requiring a payment to authenticate and unlock them.

Social technology: an attack which is based on individual interaction to deceive users to dividing security procedures to acquire sensitive information that's usually protected.

Phishing: a kind of fraud where admits mails are shipped which resemble mails from respectable sources nonetheless, the purpose of these mails would be to steal sensitive data, such as bank card or login details.

Cyber-security danger vectors

A danger Vector is really a course or way where a hacker could access a laptop or system host to supply a payload or malicious outcome. Strike vectors let hackers to exploit system vulnerabilities, for example human operators. Popular assault vectors comprise these:

- USB-Sticks and other mobile storage apparatus
- unsupported browser extensions
- infected sites
- orphan accounts
- advertisements
- online quizzes and personality tests

Components of Cyber-security

It may be A struggle in cyber-security to stay informed about the shifting security risks. The standard approach is to focus funds on key platform components. Now, ensuring cyber-security demands the coordination of efforts through the duration of a data system, which comprises these:

- Software safety: Reduce the probability that unauthorized code should find a way to govern software to get, steal, alter or delete sensitive data.
- Information security (infosec): Shield information resources, no matter how the data is structured or whether it's in transit, has been processed or has been in rest in storage.
- Network-security: Detect, prevent and respond to risks with using security policies, applications tools plus it services.
- Business continuity planning (BCP)/disaster recovery preparation (DRP): Maintain or fast restart mission-critical functions after a tragedy.
- Operational security (opsec): Classify information resources, and also determine that the controls essential to safeguard these resources.
- Enduser instruction: Supply directives that clarify what activities employees must choose -- or avoid -- so that you can secure corporate resources.

Great Things about Cyber-security

The Advantages of executing cyber-security initiatives include these:

- firm protection against malware, malware ransomware, phishing and social technologies;
- coverage for networks and data;
- avoidance of unauthorized users obtaining digital resources;
- advancement of retrieval period after a breach;
- security of end-users and also their personally identifiable information (PII); along with
- advancement of confidence from the company.

Cyber-security challenges

Cyber-security Is always contested with hackers, data loss, solitude, hazard control and changing cyber-security strategies. Nothing now indicates that cyber-attacks will fall. More over, by having an higher range of entrance points for strikes, more plans for procuring digital resources are required to shield networks and apparatus.

Certainly one of The most debatable components of cyber-security is that the always evolving nature of security risks. As new technologies emerge and current technologies is employed in fresh or unique ways, fresh paths of attack have been manufactured also. Maintaining with all these continual modifications and progress in strikes and upgrading methods to protect them against them could be hard for associations. Additionally, this includes making certain every one of the elements of cyber-security are always changed and upgraded to protect against potential vulnerabilities. This could be particularly hard for smaller businesses.

In Addition, Now, there's a whole lot of possible data a business can gather on those who get involved in another of the own services. Using an increase of data being accumulated, the odds of a cyber-criminal who would like to sneak PII is just another concern. By way of instance, a business which stores PII from the cloud could possibly be at the mercy of a ransomware attack and really should do exactly what it is to protect against a cloud violation.

Cyber-security Should additionally address cloud-based instruction, as employees can accidentally attract a virus into an office in their job computer, notebook or smartphone.

Still another Large challenge to cyber-security could be your staffing deficit. As expansion in data From companies becomes important, the demand for more cyber-security Personnel using the best required skills to test, manage and answer Episodes increases. It's estimated that there are just two million Un-filled Cyber-security projects worldwide. Cyber-security Ventures also estimated, by 2021, there'll be up to 3.5 million un-filled cyber-security jobs.

Automation

New Advances in machine-learning and artificial intelligence (AI) are increasingly being developed which help security professionals organize and manage log data. AI and machine learning can help in areas having high-volume data flows, like these:

- correlating data by coordinating it, pinpointing potential dangers and calling an attacker's following measure;
- discovering infections by implementing an security system which could analyze data and comprehend dangers;
- generating protections without putting a strain on tools; along with
- always auditing the efficacy of protections set up to guarantee they're working.

Cyber-security sellers

As a Results of raising security risks, investments in cyber-security services and technologies are climbing. Gartner forecast that global spending on information security services and products and services could hit $114 billion in 2018 and a second 8.7percent growth to $124 billion in 20-19.

Vendors In cyber-security areas will on average utilize end-point, network and complex hazard protection safety, in addition to data loss avoidance (DLP). Three well-known cyber-security vendors are Cisco, McAfee and Trend Micro. Cisco Has a tendency to concentrate on networks and empowers its clients to work with firewalls, virtual private networks (VPNs) and advanced level anti-virus security, together with encouraging email and end point security. Cisco also supports real-time malware obstructing.

McAfee Makes cyber-security services and products for consumers and enterprise clients. McAfee supports cellular telephone, enterprise clouds, network, web and Server based security. Data security and security will be also offered.

Trend Micro is a antimalware seller that features threat coverage for mobile, hybrid vehicle clouds, SaaS and the net of things (IoT). Trend Micro provides users with end-point, email and security.

Careers in Cyber-security

Whilst the Cyberthreat landscape keeps growing and new dangers emerge -- such as dangers on the landscape of IoT -- humans are expected with awareness and skills of the security hardware and applications.

IT Professionals and different household pros are wanted in security occupations, like these:

- Chief information security officer (CISO): This person implements the security application throughout the company and manages the IT security department's surgeries.
- Security Agency: This Person protects business assets from dangers having a focus on quality management over the IT infrastructure.
- Safety builder: they is in charge of planning, assessing, designing, analyzing, maintaining and encouraging a business's critical infrastructure.
- Safety analyst: they has a lot of responsibilities which have preparation security measures and

controllers, protecting digital files, and ranning both external and internal security audits.

History

Crucial Milestones in cyber-security history include these:

- Back in 1971, the creeper virus has been found; nevertheless, it really is often called the first virus.
- At 1983, Massachusetts Institute of Technology (MIT) has been awarded a patent for a cryptographic communications strategy and procedure -- that the very first cyber-security patent.
- From the 1990s, the arrival of computer viruses resulted in the disease of tens of thousands of computers (PCs), inducing cyber-security to develop into household dilemma and easing the production of antivirus program.
- Back in 1993, the initial DEFCON seminar occurred; its own attention was cyber-security.
- Back in 2003, Anonymous has been formed -- the very first renowned cookie group.
- In 2013, the Goal breach happened by which 40 million debit and credit card records were obtained and discharged.

- In 20-16, Yahoo reported two cyber-security breaches in that hackers gained access to data out of over 500 million user account.

- In 2017, the Equifax security violation happened, which exposed the personal information up to 147 million people.

- In 2018, the Typical Data Protection Legislation (GDPR) has been executed. It centered on the security of Enduser data in Europe (EU).

- Additionally in 2018, the California Consumer Privacy Act (CCPA) has been executed. It encourages individuals' right to restrain their particular PII.

- The planet is based on technology greater than ever. As a Result, digital data production has soared. Now, organizations and authorities save a excellent deal of this data on computers and also transmit it around networks into additional computers. Devices and their inherent systems have vulnerabilities which, when tapped, sabotage medical insurance and objectives of a company.

A information breach could have a Assortment of catastrophic effects For almost any business enterprise. It can interrupt a organization's standing through the increased loss of partner and consumer confidence. The increasing loss of crucial information, such as source files or intellectual property, may cost a company its competitive gain. Moving further, a data breach could influence corporate earnings as a result of noncompliance with data security regulations. It's estimated that, normally, a statistics breach costs an influenced organization $3.6 million. With high profile statistics breaches making media headlines, it's crucial that businesses embrace and execute a strong cyber-security strategy.

Shared Kinds of Cyber-security

Network-security Protects traffic by controlling incoming and outgoing links to prevent dangers from spreading or entering on the system.

Data reduction Prevention (DLP) protects information by emphasizing the location, classification and Tracking of advice whatsoever, in usage as well as in motion.

Cloud Security Provides security for data used in cloud-based applications and services.

Intrusion Detection Systems (IDS) or Intrusion Prevention Systems (IPS) work to spot potentially hostile cyber actions.

Access and Access Management (IAM) utilize authentication solutions to restrict and monitor employee accessibility to Protect internal systems from malicious things.

Encryption is the process of communicating information to leave it Unintelligible, and it is frequently used during data transport to avoid theft.

Antivirus/anti-malware providers scanning pcs for known dangers. Modern Solutions are able to find previously unknown dangers based in their behavior.

Cyber-security Is Continually Evolving

Conventional Cyber-security is focused around the execution of defensive measures around a specified perimeter. Current enablement initiatives such as distant employees and Bring Your Own Device (BYOD) policies have contradicted the perimeter, paid off visibility into cyber actions, and enlarged the strike surface.

Now, Breaches are rising at a fast pace despite recording levels of security. World-wide associations are turning into human-centric cyber-security, a fresh approach that puts concentrate on fluctuations in user behavior rather than an unspecified variety of growing dangers. Determined by behavior analytics, human-centric cyber-security offers insight to just how an end user interacts using extends and data security controls to most of the procedures where data resides, even when perhaps not entirely controlled by the company. Fundamentally, this strategy was made to spot behavioral anomalies as a way to enhance and surface the many serious dangers, reducing evaluation and hazard detection times.

Managing Cyber-security

The National Cyber-security Alliance, throughout SafeOnline.org, advocates a top-level strategy to cyber-security by which corporate direction contributes the cost in deploying cyber-security direction across all enterprise techniques. NCSA counsels that organizations have to be ready to "answer this inevitable cyber episode, reestablish normal operations, and make certain that company resources and the organization's standing are guarded." NCSA's tips for conducting cyber hazard assessments concentrate on three important areas: identifying your company's "crown jewels," or the valuable advice requiring security; pinpointing the dangers and risks facing this advice; and summarizing the harm your business would incur in case data be lost or wrongfully vulnerable. Cyber hazard assessments should even think about any regulations which impact the way in which your organization gathers, stores, and also secures data, for example as for instance pci dss, HIPAA, SOX, FISMA, along with others. Adhering to a cyber hazard assessment, develop and execute a strategy to mitigate cyber hazard, protect the"crown jewels" summarized on your appraisal, and efficiently detect and react to security events. This course of action needs to encompass the procedures and technologies needed to construct a mature cyber-security program. An ever-evolving niche, cyber-security recommendations must evolve to adapt the increasingly complex attacks carried from attackers. Mixing solid cyber-security measures having a knowledgeable and security-minded employee base supplies the very best defense against cyber-criminals trying to obtain admittance to your organization's sensitive data. While it might look to be an intimidating endeavor, start small and concentrate on your most sensitive data, increasing your time and efforts because your cyber app evolves.

A frame for enhancing Cyber-security discussions within businesses

Clear And regular communication is critical but frequently with a lack of businesses' cyber-security programs. Here is how security professionals may cause smaller bonds using some crucial stakeholders.

The Planet is moving digital; just about any sort of crossborder small business trade currently features an electronic component. Organizations' utilization of electronic technologies will be opening them up to new relationships with new clients and business partners, and also new work at home opportunities. However, as recent reports have clarified, the act of linking to the outside world increases associations' threats exponentially--of job failure, of data breach, or even worse.

In This age of World-wide digital leaks, organizations must get all probable actions to develop robust cyber-security capacities. Security strategies can't be concentrated exclusively on technical controllers and remediation plans. Firms must emphasise the individual element too. They need to want to build digitally resilient civilizations in which cyber-security isn't a occasional concern but a day to day job for heart business stakeholders in all levels, inside and outside the company. Such cultures, discussions about strength security are proactive instead of reactive, and communications one of critical decision manufacturers are available as well as frequent.

Trust among company stakeholders is a Essential element Of resilient civilizations; with no associations could have a challenging time successfully protecting the consumer data which now is indeed critical for achieving business objectives. The board should expect that senior management features a long-term perspective of cyber-security, with a tactical roadmap also plans in place to satisfactorily protect information assets and IT systems, irrespective of where and the new dangers emerge. The company components, the IT company, and also the cyber-security team have to trust the other person enough for to your mutual agreement on the way security protocols might be incorporated into daily business procedures without causing operational challenges and challenges. Businesses have to have beliefs that outside spouses --such as example, cloud vendors--are both willing and equipped to safeguard shared infrastructure and data. And government agencies will need to trust companies are reporting breaches and sharing advice which may assist them identify and thwart big cyber incident, especially those crossing numerous industries and countries or even between state-sponsored strikes.

Trust one of these stakeholders is frequently forfeited to get a Number of motives, including conflicts of interest and insufficient insight to the complicated engineering and theories related to cyber-security. When technology and business professionals do not possess a frequent comprehension of cyber-security problems, for example, they may possibly never precisely implement security protocols, and also their adoption of the most up-to-date and greatest technologies might never yield the required benefits.

In this Guide, we investigate the communication gaps that Exist one of those stakeholders, and we suggest strategies to bridge those divides. We share our perspectives concerning the dysfunctional relationships which could grow within the ecosystem, while still recognizing that the complicated trust gap still exists between organizations and clients. Certainly, no cyber-security program can be 100 percent fool proof; the threat landscape is still changing too fast. However, we believe the businesses that may ease expecting relationships and favorable discussions regarding how exactly they secure significant business assets are going to be more prepared to react to ever-advancing cyber-threats.

Trust difference 1: The plank and also the C-suite

The energetic involving board supervisors and the senior Management staff might be fraught for almost any variety of reasons, but on the list is that cyber-security is not often really a high thing on many board meeting agendas;

frequently it's presented as a part of a bigger conversation of IT problems, if it's said in any respect. Many board supervisors hence have a tendency to be informed about cyber-security engineering and problems since they are on conventional financial and operational problems --besides what they see in papers regarding the hottest corporate or government security violation. They arrive at the table together with questions in regards to the organization's cyber-security programs. For example, would be the provider's main resources being adequately shielded, and can be there a solid response-and-recovery plan set up if a violation does happen? Who owns the cyber-security schedule, also can this person or team possess the proper degree of power and sway to mobilize the necessary resources?

A hope gap develops when mature administration falls short in. Answering those questions. Sometimes, the senior management team may possibly well not have the capability to precisely opine on government problems as it's not definitely defined owners to get particular cyber-security problems and tasks such as example those who needs to manage safety training modules: the leaders at the company units, or even in IT? Even the senior management team might well not need the ideal data at your fingertips to correctly measure the recent quantities of risk the firm faces and pose a thorough reduction plan to the plank. Or the associates of this c suite simply might not keep intouch with the board regularly enough in regards to cyber-security problems: in spite of the reality that transparency is still a fresh standard in many businesses, our research shows that just 25 percent of employers present IT security upgrades into the board more often than annually, as well as 35 percent of organizations report that information only on demand.

Finding common floor

Members of those C-suite have to create more transparency and Forge stronger communicating with board supervisors. Senior leaders should officially measure the maturity in these cyber-security programs regularly and demonstrate their own findings to the board annually however rather more usually. This practice should demand a structured considerationby members of their senior-leadership group along with many others from IT and the sections, of their seriousness and probability of strikes major company resources. For Example, which inner and external dangers will be the largest, and What's the company value at stake

Through this procedure, the C-suite can develop A dash or normal reporting mechanism to alert the board about present and past degrees of danger and the possible effects of hazard on the business. Such dashboards and reports have to use clear, simple language as opposed to the acronyms usually preferred in tech discussions. Plus so they ought to include impact announcements: Exactly what would be the economic, functional, and technological consequences of emerging risks into your business enterprise? By setting routine reports regarding cyber-security, the c suite could indicate the value of this issue into the plank and the requirement to place cyber-security besides the board inspection of overall IT initiatives.

Trust gap two: The company units as well as the IT company

Trust-based relationships among people at the Small Business Units, the IT company, and also the cyber-security function might be hard to maintain simply because these groups sometimes work at cross purposes. Even the cyber-security team could inflict certain security protocols which can be inconvenient for employees available units, or impede their everyday operations. Take carefully your reactions to IT asks to improve passwords coming up with still another password with got the mandatory period and complexity and you can still remember. Such exasperation can range from the specific level to this business unit level.

(See sidebar, "Just how Wealthy development helps close the confidence difference between your small business and IT.")

For their role, Cyber-security teams can become frustrated with Business coworkers that whine about those perceived inconveniences and also don't comprehend the major role they play defending digital small business resources. When cyber-security teams provide data- and - system-access rights to employees, they need to expect that individuals will behave suitably. Even the IT group anticipates employees to become broadly knowledgeable of how corporate systems work, the way their activities online are traceable, and also how to protect their own credentials and information. However, actually, company insiders can pose substantial cyber-security risks. 1 cyber-security analytics found that 60 percent of cyberattacks at 2015 included insiders, a rise of 5 percent points from the last calendar year.

Bulking up coaching attempts

To help shut the confidence gap between the IT and Cyber-security functionality and the company, the company might offer extensive cyber-security training to staffers at all levels. This may possibly consist of dedicated townhall meetings, workshops and training modules focused on pinpointing varying kinds of cyber-threats and outlining appropriate answers when employees observe questionable activity.

Such coaching helps Business Unit employees comprehend The reason for cyber-security protocols and enhance their own awareness. Even more essential, it might indicate into the sections which cyber-security is a common responsibility. Anybody with access to private systems and data, at any level, has to play a significant part in ensuring their own safety.

Organizations Might Also Want to build up mechanisms Where IT And cyber-security professionals may discover more about the consequences of any security competitions on industry operations. For example, a few organizations are deploying a talent-factory version that motivates cyber-security professionals to do the job in different fields of the corporation in a nutshell rotations to widen their viewpoints. Their duties might be centered on learning about tech issues away from the security field as an example, network direction, center IT infrastructure, and application improvement. In a perfect world, cyber-security team associates are embedded in sections to find out more about commodity direction, public affairs and communications, or even fund. The outcome is frequently more awareness sharing and much better communication among teams.

The Cyber-security and IT groups must utilize all accessible Technologies and tools at their disposal to know as far as they could about people and procedures, hence creating more transparency regarding security problems. They ought to set clear policies representing which employees of which levels can predict that kinds of information, so when. Where permissible they could back these up coverages with a extensive identity-and-access management platform -- even a rules-based platform which automatically monitors on the web tasks, frees access rights, and also problems alarms. In addition, where permissible, they can utilize predictive analytics to spot risks until breaches can occur-- as an example, using network info and login data to recognize potentially malicious celebrities and activities in the business.

Trust difference 3: The Business and its sellers

The relationship between businesses and their technologies and also Supply chain vendors has been complex. As consumers depend on organizations to maintain their data safe and also to make use of them in a way they have licensed, organizations must expect their IT and Supply chain vendors to put up competitive information near the vest. Auto makers, for example, will have to be convinced their OEMs have enough cyber-security controllers set up to defend the intellectual property that they have been discussing.

This Is Particularly True in an age where more and much more Organizations are outsourcing the administration of the IT infrastructures or their cyber-security operations. Organizations have to rest certain that the access they offer to sellers and the offers that they purchase from vendors might be incorporated with existing systems without even opening any security holes.

Withdrawing spouses nearer

To bridge this confidence difference, business IT and company leaders Should program normal talks with sellers and Supply chain spouses to maintain the degree of security needed to safeguard shared small business info. Such meetings should happen quarterly or bi-annually; using more frequent contact, both vendors and company officials may take part in an actual business venture as opposed to the usual simple transactional relationship. They could talk and invent clear recovery and reimbursement plans.

Organizations can take it a step farther by actively Cooperating with third-party providers and Supply chain spouses to make sure adequate data security. They could collectively pursue security certificates, like the Payment Card Industry Data Security Standard or the ISO 27001 conventional, or ran combined inspections and safety instructions of IT systems. They could even consent to open up themselves to and including broader ecosystem of technology partners to offer extra checks and accounts.

For their role, tech sellers may include terms Inside their service-level arrangements, for example, for regaining restoring or data system accessibility within designated timeframes. Or they could agree to give insurance to pay virtually any firm the provider loses as a consequence of an attack within owner's approaches. Most insurance companies have started to add cyber incidents in their actuarial tables. Even the common coverage now continues to be narrow, however these coverages may possibly turn into the next tool vendors and Supply chain spouses may use in order to guarantee organizations they have been increasingly being shielded against cyber-attack -- consequently shutting the confidence difference.

Trust gap 4: The Business and the authorities

It is Not Surprising That local, nationwide, and national Authorities have in modern times motivated private sector businesses to be much more mindful of cyber-security problems and more busy within their Data protection efforts. Cyber-attacks in major finance institutions may impact entire economy equilibrium. Energy-grid hacks can pose federal dangers, too, even as we heard from the new attempted break-ins at twelve power plants at the USA. Government agencies want organizations to report cyber-attacks and other events in a timely manner, as a way to fortify capillary protection efforts--such as example, spotting and fixing questionable patterns of activity and alerting the populace to some threats.

Seeing the large image

Neither side can afford to combat cyber-attacks by itself. Businesses want the state imprimatur and gravitas that government agencies may offer as facilitators of both cyber-security analyses and negotiations of sensitive details. Authorities require the feedback and technical tools which private sector businesses may offer.

Around the Planet, governments are taking measures to encourage Organizations' developments with their own cyber-security programs. The federal government of Australia hosts annual cyber-security leadership meetings, at which in fact the prime minister and enterprise leaders establish plan for strengthening cyber-security efforts in the public and private industries. And the federal government of Singapore has also established a collection of people - and - private sector collaborations created to fortify the nation's capacities in cyber-security research.

For their own part, some businesses believe that there are ways to Further enhance public-private ventures. 1 main information security officer in a international bank mentioned the requirement to expand the federal detection system. A CIO at a financial services firm urged for greater sharing of technical intelligence. "Thus far, there are just a couple discussion geared toward businesses that are specific. It isn't enough for some organizations," he told.

CHAPTER TWO
ROLES AND RESPONSIBILITIES

Our private and professional lives are connected by Technology in ways which were unthinkable only a couple decades past. The cloud computing, freedom, and also the powerful devices the majority folks possess inside our pockets empower a culture of advantage, and also the capacity to collaborate and become more efficient. While this benefit arguably creates our own lives easier, in addition, it makes it a lot easier for cyber-criminals to acquire access to our own sensitive individual information wherever it resides or where it's traveling throughout the system. These terrible actors possess considerable motivation, too -- there exists a flourishing market for your selling and manipulation of this data. Despite having most useful cyber-security Professional in your own side, hackers and cyber-criminals will sooner or later find a solution to arrive at your own data. That is certainly not to imply all is impossible, nevertheless. IT security specialists Work with front lines of the struggle fighting to shield against the always evolving threat landscape

Functions of their Cyber-security Professional

At a Milehigh degree, Cyber-security professionals are In charge of protecting IT infrastructure, border networks, devices, and data. More granularly, they're liable for preventing data breaches and observation and responding to strikes. Some have backgrounds as developers, and network or systems administrators, as well as in mathematics and statistics. Those skills are definitely related to this use of an IT security professional, however quite critical would be things which are not necessarily matters which can be educated -- critical thinking, curiosity, and a passion for research and learning. People from all types of backgrounds possess the qualities, therefore organizations should not confine themselves to a pool of applicants. Further, most hackers are creative with nature. To out smart them, security experts will need to be, too.

Responsibilities of this Cyber-security Professional

New safety threats Appear All of the time, and IT security Professionals will need to remain current with the most recent approaches hackers ' are applying in the area. Along with this high tech duties Mentioned Previously, a few special responsibilities IT security groups perform, comprise:

- Establish and execute user access controls and identity and access management methods
- Monitor system and program performance to Spot and intermittent action
- Perform routine audits to Guarantee safety practices are compliant
- Deploy End Point detection and avoidance tools to successfully repel malicious hacks
- Put up limitation management methods to upgrade software mechanically
- Implement comprehensive vulnerability management methods across all resources on-premises and at the cloud
- Assist IT operations to Prepare a shared catastrophe recovery/business allocation strategy
- Use HR and/or staff attempts to instruct workers on the Best Way to identify questionable activity
- Three Critical Skills for Cyber-security Professionals
- Successful IT security pros want longer than Technical abilities. To genuinely progress in the area, these pros should be:

- Strategists - Cyber-security professionals will really be able to implement security controls and measures within associations, considering the implications of any actions. Advanced level security protocols need strategic and tactical ratings of workflows, dependencies, budgets, and tools. Because new procedures to hack on information are continuously growing, professionals have to be considered a step ahead, analyzing how hackers input procedures and networks to thwarting them.

- Communicators - Direction and communicating skills ensure successful communication with clients and teams. Tech and security contact each professional in a business. Security professionals must interact in meaningful ways with training and empowering employees to help protect approaches.

- Lifelong Learners - Still another must have skill is technical proficiency. With the pace of development inside security, what this means is ongoing training, research, and getting standard certificates. These professionals should always be learning new higher level technical skills in order to eliminate complex security problems.

- Cyber Dangers are chilling. Not merely are they really complex and always evolving, but they will have the capability to impart substantial financial and reputational injury to a organization. Plus, there is absolutely no solution to be 100 percent secure. This is exactly why cyber-security is not any longer only the responsibility of IT sections. Boards of Managers are responsible and responsible to the success of their own organizations, and also in the modern connected environment, cyber durability is large portion of this responsibility. Which usually means that Boards must have a dynamic part in cyber-security.

As Boards Of Directors undertake the function of cyber-security leaders of their associations, below are a few responsibilities they must look into.

Board of Managers Responsibilities

The National Association of Corporate Directors (NACD)," Director's Handbook about Cyber-Risk Oversight summarizes five fundamentals which corporate boards must look into" since they want to boost their supervision of cyber dangers."

- Trainers will need to know and approach cyber-security being an enterprise-wide hazard control issue, not simply an IT issue.   Just as we've been mentioning that, it's surprising just how many businesses still connect information security or cyber-security using IT. Despite the fact that the majority of the coverage arrangements come up throughout the IT section, it can not be the fundamental focus since the consequences are organization-wide. Even the skillsets necessary to handle the risks and treat problems are organization-wide. The Board should realize a 1:1 using it really is an error, which has been the underlying reason behind several huge violation events.

- Managers ought to comprehend the regulatory and legal consequences of cyber threats because they relate for their own corporation's specific conditions. With responsibility comes responsibility. Executive board and management members are now being held liable for most visible breaches, as well as oftentimes losing their rankings. Target CEO, President and Chairman Gregg Steinhafel resigned all of his rankings subsequent to the Large 2013 information breach. And Much More recently, Equifax's CEO Richard Smith stepped after a backlash within the gigantic hack that jeopardized the information of estimated 143 million Americans.

- Boards needs to have sufficient accessibility to cyber-security expertise, and discussions relating to cyber-risk direction needs to be provided routine and sufficient time on the Board meeting schedule. It's getting more prevalent to visit Board members who have a technical or safety background. This expertise can definitely raise a Boards' comprehension. And much more awareness is the way we triumph against cyber-criminals.

- Directors have to place the expectation that direction will set a enterprise-wide hazard management frame together with sufficient staffing and funds. The NACD handbook expressly cited the National Institute of Standards and Technology cyber-security framework (NIST CSF), that is made to empower" associations -- no matter of size, amount of cyber-security hazard or cyber-security elegance -- to apply the fundamentals and best methods of risk management to improving the durability and security of critical infrastructure" Once you are writing your coverages or developing a schedule, acquiring a frame to base it is extremely beneficial. There is absolutely no need to reinvent the wheel!

- Board-management talk of cyber hazard will consist of identification which risks in order to avert, accept, mitigate, or even move through insurance, in addition to special plans connected with each approach. Effortlessly managing cyber-security hazard demands an awareness of the comparative importance of organizational resources as a way to ascertain the frequency through which they'll soon be scrutinized for hazard outages. That is no little endeavor. It will take substantial effort and thought, together side a excellent deal of cyber-security expertise.

Regulatory Guidance and Conditions

Longer Cyber-mature businesses have regulatory guidance and requirements in regards to the cyber-security responsibilities of this Board of Managers. Let us look at the financial / banking market. The Federal Financial Institutions Examination Council (FFIEC) urges handbooks to direct their examiners and auditors within the area. According to those handbooks, here is what examiners expect you'll locate.

Board Responsibilities -- This App

The Board Of Directors sets the direction and tone for the institution's usage of IT. The Board should accept the IT strategic program, data protection program, and Additional

IT-related policies. The Board or a Board committee ought to function the After:

- Inspection and accept IT Strategic plan that aligns with the overall enterprise plan.
- Boost powerful IT governance.
- Oversee procedures for Approving the institution third-party providers.
- Oversee and Get upgrades On important IT projects, IT budgets, IT priorities, along with entire IT performance.
- Oversee the adequacy and Allocation of IT tools for financing and employees.
- Approve coverages to innovate And report substantial security events to the Board of Managers.
- Hold management accountable For measuring, identifying, and mitigating IT threats.
- Give impartial, Comprehensive, and efficient audit policy of IT controls.

Board Responsibilities -- Audit

- The board and senior management are accountable for making sure the organization's system of internal controllers works effortlessly.

- The Board of Managers should make sure that written instructions for ranning IT audits are embraced.
- The Board or its own audit committee is in charge of approving and reviewing audit plans (like programs and policies), and tracking the efficacy of the audit role.

Board Responsibilities -- Third-party Service Providers

The Financial institution Board and senior management needs to set and accept risk-based policies to regulate the outsourcing procedure. The policies have to recognize the danger of this organization by outsourcing relationships and needs to really be appropriate to the magnitude and complexity of the institution. Facets associations must look into include:

- Assessing each and every outsourcing relationship affirms the organization's entire requirements and tactical aims.
- Strengthening the organization has adequate expertise to manage and control the relationship.
- Assessing prospective providers dependent on the extent and criticality of services that are outsourced.

- Tailoring the enterprise-wide, service-provider monitoring application based on initial and ongoing hazard evaluations of services that are outsourced.
- Notifying its main ruler seeing outsourced relationships, when demanded by this ruler.
- The Function of Cyber-security Inside the Organization
- Generally Speaking, Cyber-security is a subset of Advice Security direction which specializes in digital data and electronic resources. Cyber-security's aim is to guarantee that the CIA of electronic information within the company. CIA represents: Confidentiality, Integrity & Availability.

To Achieve this type of Cyber-security strategy needs:
- Establish safety dimensions & metrics
- keep knowledge of emerging threats & vulnerabilities
- Translate risks into business effect for Sr. direction
- Recommend Best-practices & sway the associations coverage, criteria, processes and Recommendations
- Make compliance with authorities and business associations

The Downline engaged Cyber-security:

Cyber-security is really a function of direction which rolls Every feature of the company. For that reason, everyone on the team gets a certain amount of participation. But, you'll find fundamental roles and responsibilities and each plays a valuable role.

C level / Sr.. Direction

C Level Accounts for producing value Decisions predicated on cyber-security vulnerability and company hazard. They got the greatest ability, so they will have the supreme responsibility for consequences of their associations cyber-security program.

Steering Committee

The Steering committee reflects the Various sections within the company. The committee's intention is to give insight into business operations, data classification, and general effect of cyber-security policy's and procedures.

Auditors

Auditors are out advisers or Authorities tasked with analyzing cyber vulnerability and hazard. It's essential that auditors aren't satisfied using the IT company, but instead of surgeries or fund.

Data Owner

Data owner -- that the information owner is In charge of its classification of information. Classification compels the company's cyber-security controllers. (General usage data might be about a document server along with some other authenticated network user may get it. Top secret information Goes into a Secure and just the COO and CFO understand the positioning of this Secure and also the lock mix)

Data Custodian

The information custodian is responsible for The secure custody, storage, transport of this data. In other words, data custodians are accountable to its technical environment and database arrangement.

Network Admin

The system admin guarantees accessibility of tools and also contains Usage of resources centered on pre-established policy and could create changes within his universe of accessibility.

Security Admin

Security Admin has access to all Allowing her to audit and quantify cyber-security efficacy. However, an security admin must have no consent to make some changes.

It is very important to note that the network admin and also the Security admin functions frequently struggle together. At the center, a system admin wishes in order to guarantee usage of resources. An security admin by comparison seeks to apply a principle of least privilege (Access to some want to know basis.) Hence these functions have to get separated. The security admin and also the system admin shouldn't be exactly the exact same individual.

CHAPTER TWO
CYBER-SECURITY ESSENTIALS

Conventional Cyber-security is based round the execution of defensive measures round a specified perimeter. Current enablement initiatives for example distant employees and Bring Your Own Device (BYOD) policies have deciphered the perimeter, paid off visibility into cyber actions, and enlarged the strike surface.

Now, Breaches are rising at a fast pace despite recording levels of security. World-wide associations are turning into human-centric cyber-security, a fresh approach that puts concentrate on fluctuations in user behavior rather than an unspecified variety of growing dangers. Determined by behavior analytics, human-centric cyber-security offers insight to the way the end user interacts using extends and data security controls to most of the procedures where data resides, even when perhaps not entirely controlled by the company. Fundamentally, this strategy was made to spot behavioral anomalies as a way to enhance and surface the many serious dangers, reducing evaluation and hazard detection times.

Cyber-security Essentials was created to give a summary of A variety of regions of the cyber-security market. Students will begin with learning basic os info, Linux security, along with Windows security. Students will move into more specific issues, such as cryptography, honeypots, Internet shield and strikes, SIEMs, security policies, and community scan. You may even learn various tools for password-cracking and also be provided a high level summary of cloud security. The greatest effect of the training course is to present students an extensive learning experience which eases them towards a cyber-security career course of their own choosing.

Cyber-security Essentials begins off with an introduction to Operating systems and virtualization. Students then determine basic networking concepts as well as also the fundamentals of both Windows and Linux security. The route then reverted to a conversation on tracking network traffic along with strategies to guard data. Students will find out about wireless networks, scanning programs using programs such as NMAP, and acting traffic sniffing using programs such as Wireshark and TCPDump. A succinct summary of cloud security principles is provided, and students subsequently learn about hazard policies and management. Students then proceed in the Internet and discover about honeypots and Internet surveillance together with the OWASP Top. Demonstrations using password cracking tools John The Ripper and Cain and Abel are up next and students are introduced into APT classes. Students then understand episode management and wrap this up class using Powershell scripting and basic details about Secure Coding.

Based Into the Ponemon Institute's 20-16 cyber-security Trends Report, 66 percentage of business and tech professionals surveyed identified as phishing and social technologies as top dangers. This must not be surprising, even as phishing and social technologies are chief resources of malware infiltration like ransom-ware.

Commonly, Social engineering entails email or alternative communication which amuses the receiver by tricking them to providing use of a type of account, login, or monetary details. Additional procedures of ingress to get cyber-attacks can originate from darkness IT, that will be UN sanctioned software utilized by employees or sections without IT's knowledge.

Certainly, The individual element is frequently the most commonplace weakness which organizations have in regards to cyber-security. While authentic end-to-end cyber-security is a continuing and constant energy to keep 1 step in front of risks, listed here are 10 cyber-security essentials which each firm will need to possess as a base.

1. Application Whitelisting

If it Involves darkness IT, the Cloud Security Alliance (CSA) Cloud Adoption methods & Priorities Survey Report discovers that a lot of organizations are aware of 38 percentage of cloud software being used inside their own businesses. Initiating application whitelisting is really a best practice for ensuring only selected computer software applications ran using computers and all others have been ceased as a member of malware avoidance.

Whitelisting Could be done with higher level application management programs, that ought to be fortified with restricting administrative statements to stop unauthorized applications in conducting. Like many fundamental cyber-security approaches for organizations, whitelisting can be just a blend of technology and policy tools, that encompasses the majority of the cyber-security essentials with this particular list.

2. Multi-Factor Authentication

Implementing Multi-factor authentication (MFA) goes beyond consideration passwords. That is attained with the addition of stronger elements like a passphrase or PIN, either a physical token or applications certification, or biometric information such as a fingerprint scan.

3. Restrict Administrative Privileges

By Restricting administrative statements to simply the employees who want them, organizations can provide a greater degree of security. This works Together with MFA.

4. Timely and consistent Application and OS Patch Management

Consistently And completely patch software and systems once they are available as a way to expel vulnerabilities to objective computers. This usually means implementing IT processes that ensure systems and software on most servers are always upgraded.

5. Disable Un-trusted Microsoft Office Macros

Disable Un-trusted Microsoft Office macros by minding Office settings to obstruct macros on the net and just enable spring-loaded macros. This gets rid of a frequent ingress attack procedure and works in combination with patch administration.

6. User Application Hardening

User friendly Application functions such as blocking web browser usage of Adobe Flash Player (un-install when potential), web advertising, along with untrusted Java code online are all area of protecting the system and also make next-generation firewalls better.

7. Employ Next-generation Firewalls

Next-generation Firewalls (NGFW) are system security systems which could detect and prevent complicated attacks by enforcing security policies at the application form, interface, and protocol degree. All these firewalls Assemble:

- Packet filtering
- Network address translation
- URL obstructing
- Virtual private networks (VPNs)
- Quality of Service (QoS) performance
- SSL and SSH review
- Deep-packet review
- Reputation-based malware detection
- Application consciousness

8. Employ a SIEM Solution

Even though This can be overkill for smaller sized organizations, at a certain point of network development, a small business should absolutely implement a security information and event management (SIEM) alternative for constant incident response and detection. This collection of incorporated technologies empowers real-time set and historical analytics of security incidents over a wide selection of sources.

9. Backup and Retrieval

Daily Backup of crucial data is essential to protecting against ransom-ware along with other malware which could reestablish corrupt, corrupted, or delete copies which may be accessible. While an everyday backup is vital, in addition, it expects that the backup has been disconnected from the system and be periodically analyzed to be sure the data will likely soon be accessible if required.

10. Penetration Testing

By Creating practices and policies for conducting routine penetration tests and vulnerability tests, organizations can identify and procure potential points of failure within and outside the system.

While maybe not As section of this listing of cyber-security essentials, employee protocols and training are all vital to making sure the individual section of protecting against hazard intrusion will probably succeed. Including everything from how to prevent malicious emails to password and device administration. By making cyber-security component of the everyday culture of the small business, associations may prevent a number of their very frequently made intrusions and much more readily accommodate by teaching their employees on emerging risks and how to safeguard them against.

A company's communication stations are frequently the Primary point of call to get the attack, delivered via spam, malicious efforts or benefiting of obsolete applications now as organizations proceed to the cloud, then this allows a second route for attack.

Just How do your company place sufficient barriers set up to Make sure it is shielded from the most recent cyber-security dangers?

Listed below are just six pointers to bear in mind when Trying to create UC security fit for this purpose.

Keeping a Formidable CMDB

Keeping a solid, well-maintained, and more powerful Configuration Database (CMDB) is just a problem for many organizations. Many businesses don't keep up their CMDB and also this makes executing security controls and processes harder and time-consuming, encouraging opening and mistakes the organization to strike.

Employ clear obligations and possession of your CMDB and Keep equipment current. The greater handled it's, the more easier dangers are to prevent. Doing so is very essential if updating infrastructure and also for people in transition of modernising your workplace.

Continual Inspection and Optimisation of this Information Security Management System (ISMS)

Continued care and inspection would be the key to making a Well-oiled machine which won't neglect as it takes to carry out. Continually examine and reevaluate your ISMS including security policies and procedures and security change management control and inspection of the hazard register. Fix these on a normal basis in accordance with current threats and vulnerabilities.

Commitment to the Most Effective Management

Frequently senior managers are focused on purposes additional Than cyber-security. They're oriented to company profits, financial effects, and much more, but frequently would not need some fantastic insight into the risks that lie at a feeble cyber-security procedure.

Fantastic cyber protection needs financial assets to fasten The infrastructure and adequate staff to deal with the procedure. These costs are usually not viewed as a requisite, particularly when they're not emphasized after budgeting.

All risks should be introduced to the senior administration of this Company, together with the effects in the event the security is violated, for example a solid assessment of the monetary consequences of a violation, in addition to the reputational damage it'll cost in the opinion of consumers. Together with up to one in four clients saying They would not be able to expect a organization after a Cyberattack, the reputational cost is Very Likely to be large

Crisis and Incident Management

Security disasters Aren't an exclusion but Instead a guideline, and Any security episode is an expected emergency if it's not processed correctly.

Incidents could be categorized with Various priorities Based upon the protentional effect. It's rather necessary that the distinctive priorities are precisely clarified and the employees who process these are well trained to offer a timely, correct and thorough reaction.

Security management methods create different types of Reports that individuals can employ to examine the cyber-security vulnerabilities inside the organization and also to take remedial actions and figure out the danger of the provider.

All Priority 1 and two episodes in Unify, as an Example, are Presented to the senior management regularly, and also every single 4 or 3 episode is escalated into a higher degree if it isn't closed in a definite period. Response time for different priorities need to be computed according to the circumstance of this organization and its own strengths and capacities, however in any situation, once the episode is priority inch the most reaction period is a few hours.

With this procedure to Work, we turn into the CMDB theme. Additionally, there are GDPR consequences if those problems aren't increased in the right interval and may lead to penalties up to $10 million, or 2 percent of annual worldwide turnover -- whatever is higher.

When WannaCry and Melt-down hit on the marketplace that the CMBD subject Was emphasized, in terms of several organizations that they had to gather all resources that have to be updated was more compared to true remediation time. It's not unusual to obtain a certain advantage without clear ownership, notably in lager businesses, and also this may pose a severe dilemma when specific action have to be obtained within hours of a cyber attack.

A catastrophe suggests an dangerous and unstable situation Associated with a massive region of the business or even the company as a complete, potentially harmful company to a excellent extent, and also requiring the commencement of minute actions. Alas, a lot of businesses would not need an optimized emergency management procedure and staff training procedures.

Finest practice dictates that all Has to Be obviously Documented, emergency management is directed by an associate of their senior management group, also that clubs meet regularly to upgrade actions and activity parts.

The Business may also have external partners to consult with Throughout a emergency situation, like a cyber-security pro, or governmental firm with which to cooperate as a way to perfect the catastrophe faster, and this also should be deducted in.

Do Not Only Stay Glued to ISO

The majority of famous safety criteria or frameworks Aren't Reactively designed and don't guarantee well-designed ISMS. ISO 27001 is an ordinary that main usage is predictive safety hazard evaluation, treatment and mitigating but comprises many risk factors by it self.

Adding Best-practices with No concrete technologies, Design or procedures demanded, and describing procedures which encircle too much confidence on the individual element from ISMS, ISO 27001 will render many additional questions and openings within a organizations cyber-security capacities.

National Institute of Standards and Technology (NIST) Frame-work

The steps shown within this frame are Identify, Protect, Detect, Respond and Recover. However, placement "Identify" as measure one way that the frame approach might be categorized as a responsive just solution. "Respond" and "Recover" additionally result in the responsive nature.

List"Identify" at the Start of cycle indicates Activities are launched just in the event of business sway. "Planning" isn't just a component with the high tech structure and certainly will be a critical measure for proactive measures or in wanting to predict upcoming troubles.

Very good procedures should comprise more transparent, organized, And fast-working cyber-security systems. Planning can also be essential. Fantastic security officials shouldn't await a matter to enhance their security or even to close themselves within boundaries of predefined standards such as ISO 27001.

Alternatively, they want to program every day, have the ability to react to Various surroundings, and generate a cyber-security focused civilization round the whole enterprise. Should they really do this right, then a business can provide itself the very greatest chance to shield itself against the following WannaCry.

What's Your Dark Web?

The dark Web identifies encoded online content that's not indexed by traditional search engines like google. Also called the"darknet," the darkened web is really a part of the profound web that refers to the wider variety of articles that doesn't seem through routine internet browsing tasks.

Specific browsers such as Tor have to get dim net Websites, that comprise anonymous community forums, online market places such as medication, trades for stolen private and financial data, and also other prohibited content. Transactions within this hidden market in many cases are taken care of with Bitcoin, and physiological goods are regularly sent in a way that cloak both sellers and buyers out of the attentive eyes of police force.

The way a Dark Web Works

The dim net has become an Internet market for prohibited goods. A number of the creations from valid online sellers such as Amazon and eBay, such as customer reviews and seller evaluations, have now been shown to ease the earnings of black market things.

The dim net attracts users that search anonymity when Conducting company. Intentions could be more commendable, for example just like journalists trying to interview citizens of all repressive nations, where communications have been tracked. The anonymity of this darkened web attracts criminal celebrities such as drug dealers, hackers, along with child porn peddlers. There's also a growing service market within the darkened web by which hit-men and other prohibited operatives advertise their services in a way they might not over conventional stations.

Dark Web Versus Deep Web

The dim net and also the profound net are usually wrongly utilized interchangeably. To describe: that the profound web comprises all of the pages which do not pop up once you conduct a internet search. This covers all demanding a login, such as personal email, online banking, online banking, or other similar websites. Conversely, the darkened web is dependent upon encryption to maintain irrefutably content anonymous.

Particular Factors

How Big this Dark Web Market

In 2016, the Economist noted the medication action fueled by the shadowy net grew From roughly $17 million in 2012 roughly $180 million in 2015. But these are mere estimations, whilst the nature of this darkened web would make it hard to accurately measure the market it supports, for example gun earnings and other prohibited trades.

Regulating the Dark World-wide Web

Regulators have fought to suppress black web action. Subsequent to the dark web drug market called Silk Road was shot down by the FBI at 2013, Silk Road two appeared and instantly flourished, before FBI and Europol closed down it in 2014. But, Silk Road 3 appeared shortly afterwards.

Along with this problem in shutting down shadowy net Market places, the technology has now evolved to the stage at which that the OpenBazaar open source code permits decentralized market places, like the way in which torrents permit searchable filesharing. Consequently, the dark online market keeps growing, despite police force's very best efforts.

What's the Typical Data protection Legislation (GDPR)?

The Overall Data protection Legislation (GDPR) Is a legal platform which sets guidelines for its processing and collection of personal advice from those who reside from the European Union (EU). Since the Legislation applies irrespective of where internet sites are established, it has to be heeded by many websites which draw European people, even when they do not specifically promote services or goods into EU residents.

The GDPR mandates which EU traffic Get Numerous data disclosures. The website also needs to take action to ease such EU consumer rights because a timely notification in case of personal data being broken. Adopted in April 20-16, the Legislation came into full effect in might 2018, after having a yearlong transition span.

Customer service Requirements of this GDPR

Under the principles, people need to be informed of information that the Website Collects out of their store and explicitly agree to this information gathering, by clicking an Agree button along with alternative actions. (This condition chiefly explains the omnipresent existence of disclosures that internet sites collect "cookies" small files which carry private information like site preferences and settings)

Internet sites also needs to notify people in a timely manner when some one of Their private data stored by the website is breached. All these EU requirements might be more rigorous than those demanded from the jurisdiction by that the website is located.

Additionally mandated is the assessment of the site's information safety, And if a passionate data security officer (DPO) has to become hired or an present staffer can take out this job.

Information on How Best to get into the DPO along with other applicable Staffers have to be reachable so that people can practice their EU data rights, and which also incorporate the means to possess their own presence on the internet site erased, along with other measures. (Obviously, the website has to add staff as well as additional tools in order of carrying such requests)

Additional Requirements and Mandates of this Typical Data protection Legislation (GDPR)

As additional protection for customers, the GDPR additionally predicts For just about any personally identifiable information (PII) that internet sites collect to be anonymized (rendered anonymous, and since the word implies) or pseudonymized (with all the customer's identity exchanged using a pseudonym). Even the pseudonymization of data allows firms to accomplish a bit broader data analytics, like analyzing average credit score of its clients in a given region--a data which may otherwise be outside the first purposes of data accumulated for analyzing credit worthiness for financing.

The GDPR affects data outside that accumulated from clients. Most importantly, perhaps, the law pertains to the individual funds' recordings of employees.

Controversies Connected with the GDPR

The GDPR has drawn criticism in certain areas. The Necessity to hone DPOs, or simply just to measure the demand for these, several state, imposes an undue administrative burden on a few organizations. Some even complain that the instructions are too vague how to take care of employee data.

Additionally, information Can't be moved to a different Nation Beyond the EU, unless your receiving company guarantees exactly the exact same level of security since the EU requires. This has caused complaints regarding high priced disturbance to industry clinics.

There is a Additional concern that the prices related to GDPR will rise overtime, simply due to the escalating necessity to educate clients and employees equally concerning data security dangers and remedies. Additionally there is uncertainty over the way feasibly data security bureaus throughout the EU and beyond may align their authorities and interpretation of regulations, and therefore assure an even playing field whilst the GDPR switches into more fuller effect.

Whatever You Want to Understand About GDPR, the Brand New Data Law
While laws and regulations are often lengthy, dull and Full of complicated jargon, some are crucial to comprehend since they might indirectly or directly affect your routine life. 1 such key law which may take effect on May 25 could be your General Data protection Legislation (GDPR). This report acts as a fast guide that will help readers comprehend its consequences.

At Short, GDPR is laws aimed at providing the End user the best to restrain their own data. As soon as it's implemented from the European Union (EU), it's farreaching consequences for major tech firms that operate worldwide. They comprise famous brands face-book Inc. (FB) and also Alphabet Inc.'s Google (GOOGL) businesses which hold massive troves of user data and also put it to use for bringing in their revenue.

GDPR Basics

GDPR Means General Data protection Legislation, a law Approved in April 20-16. It supersedes a previous law known as the Data Protection Directive and it is geared toward distributing the rules over the full EU region. GDPR let organizations two years to follow the essential alterations.

As a Growing Number of businesses, particularly those from the Technology industry, keep to assemble loads of users' personal data, both the management and control of all user data eventually lies at the control of these businesses. After that it becomes more likely to use (and abuse) of those organizations, their employees, and also at risk of hacks. GDPR tries to provide users the charge of their private information. The judgment are also related to businesses that are established outside the EU, however, offer services or products to EU clients. This really is why global businesses are concerned and therefore are reluctant to abide by the regulation.

The Intricacies of GDPR

Currently, one needs to Click on the "I Agree" button On a page that's packed with complex and jargon that are open-ended. It's not simply obscure and difficult to comprehend, but in addition allows businesses to seek out user approval for anything they need. For example, buying a toy out of an e-commerce portal could involve sharing a single' delivery address along with contact number, however hidden under the very long set of terms and requirements might be a requirement which permits the portal site to talk about those details together with entrepreneurs.

GDPR is set to change everything. It can make it hard For those businesses to use obscure, benign and confusing vocabulary to really have an individual accept anything they need.

Currently, There's No clarity concerning the way the business handles A consumer's data when an individual withdraws in their own services. As an example, there are factors that if a user occupies a social networking account, the business might maintain their details indefinitely.

GDPR delivers the necessary "directly to be forgotten," so the provider, in addition to any affiliated entities together with your computer data, will probably be asked to divert it out of their own records.

GDPR additionally supplies for Simple lack of approval any Point intime. For under age users, people under 16, eligible defender (s) would need to give permission in the behalf for data collection.

Users may even Have the Ability to Understand the exact data points Being saved, and where and is the company together. GDPR lets for data integration -- which is, end users may simply take their data and move it into some other provider. A potential execution of the data portability is whenever a user wants to proceed from google plus into facebook, or by 1 online rental agency into one other, which makes the procedure simpler.

Any information Breaches will finally need to be reported on the concerned government within 72 hrs of their organization becoming conscious of it. Likewise users will even have to be advised of such violation with no undue delay. Currently, without a clarity on the deadline of intimation, lots of organizations hit by hacking efforts and also data stealth maintain the events hidden indefinitely.

Effect on Firms

The law stipulates penalties that are monetary in Case GDPR legislation have been broken. A strong can be levied a fine up to 4 percent of its entire worldwide turnover in the event there is any GDPR offenses, and with a minimal group in 20 million euros (roughly $24.5 million). With major technology firms having earnings in billions, some offenses will throw a major effects.

Whilst the two-year execution interval is almost over And the go-live deadline is coming to a close, people happen to be seeing with a flurry of alarms within their own inbox from several providers in regards to the upgraded policy fluctuations. On the list of significant firms, facebook has recently released a few privacy-oriented programs and Google has upgraded its own policy across number of its solutions.

What's a Data Breach?

A information breach (also Called data spill or information Flow) is a unauthorized access and recovery of sensitive information via a person, group, or applications system. It's a cyber-security accident which occurs when data, intentionally or intentionally, falls to the incorrect hands minus the wisdom of the owner or user.

Wearing down Data Breach

Data breaches are partially caused by this climbing Accessibility of data as a result of gain of digital services and products, that includes put together an overwhelming level of information from the control of organizations. While a number of these info is non sensitive, many it is sensitive and proprietary information regarding companies and individuals. The concentrate on technology-driven tools like Cloud computing platforms also has made information easily accessible, readily reachable, and readily shareable for modest expenses. Organizations use and share this data to better their procedures and meet up with the requirements of a growing tech savvy populace. But some miscreants try to acquire access for the info as a way to utilize it for prohibited activities. The gain in the episodes of data breaches listed within businesses throughout the entire world has attracted to the spotlight the matter of cyber-security and data solitude, that includes generated lots of regulatory bodies dilemma new legislation to combat.

Users and owners of a busted network or system do not Always know instantly as soon as the violation happened. In 20-16, Yahoo declared what Might be the largest cyber-security breach nonetheless if it maintained an estimated

500-million balances were broken. Additional analytics revealed that the Data breach had actually happened a couple of decades before in 2014.

Although Some Cyber-criminals use stolen information to Frighten Or extort money from businesses and individuals, the others sell the broken information in subterranean web market places which transaction in prohibited resources. Cases of information which are bought and sold from such dark webs comprise stolen credit card info, industry intellectual property, SSN, along with company trade secrets.

Unintentional Data Breach

A information breach could be performed out Inadvertently or intentionally. An accidental data breach happens when the best custodian of all details like a worker falls or negligently uses corporate programs. A member of staff that accesses private sites, downloads a compromised applications application on a job notebook, joins into a unsecured wi-fi system, loses a notebook or smartphone at a public place, etc.. conducts the possibility of experiencing his corporation's data deciphered. Back in 2015," Nutmeg, an internet expenditure management business, needed its statistics endangered once a faulty code from your machine led in e-mailing the personally identifiable information (PII) of all 3 2 accounts into the receivers. The info which has been sent outside contained addresses, names, and investment information and place the accounts holders in danger of identity-theft.

Intentional Data Breach

An deliberate data breach occurs when a cyberattacker Hacks to someone's or company's system with the intention of accessing personal and proprietary info. Cyber hackers make use of various tactics to enter a method. A few imbed malicious applications from email or websites attachments which, once obtained, create the computer vulnerable to easy accessibility and entry of information from hackers. Many hackers use bot-nets , that can be infected computers to get into other servers' files. Bot-nets permit the perpetrators to acquire admittance to multiple servers at precisely the exact same time working with exactly the exact same malware application. Hackers can also start using a source chain attack to gain access info. If a business has a great and impenetrable security step set up, a hacker can go through an associate of the provider's distribution chain system with a susceptible security technique. Once the user gets into the penis's computer system he could possibly obtain access into this prospective company's network too.

Hackers do not need to steal sensitive info such as Social Security Numbers (SSN) simultaneously to show a consumer's identity and gain use of their profile. In the instance of concealing information for identity theft, hackers using data collections of quasi-identifiers can patch together items of advice to show the identity of a thing. Quasi-identifiers such as gender, age, marital status, race, and speech can be had from other origins and pieced together to get a individuality. In 2015, the IRS confirmed a statistics breach of over 300,000 tax-payers had happened. The cyber offenders had used quasi-identifiers to obtain the citizens' advice and fill in tax refund software. This caused the IRS doling around $50 million in paychecks into the identity thieves.

CHAPTER THREE
CYBER-SECURITY AND HACKING

In case You've ever researched famous conflicts ever, you will recognize that no 2 will be exactly alike. Still, you will find definite plans and approaches usually utilized in conflict as they're time-proven to work.

Similarly, If an offender is seeking to hack on organization, they won't re invent the wheel till they have to: They will draw up on ordinary kinds of hacking methods which can be understood to be extremely effective, such as malware, phishing, or even cross-site scripting (XSS). Whether you are attempting to make awareness of the hottest data breach mantra from the news headlines or assessing a incident on your organization, it will help to comprehend different attack vectors a malicious celebrity may possibly attempt to cause injury. Here is an summary of a number of the very typical kinds of attacks found now.

Cyber-security Identifies the measures required to keep private information confidential and protected against theft or damage. It's also utilized to create sure that these data and devices aren't misused. Cyber-security pertains to both hardware and software, in addition to info online, and may be used to protect from personal info to complex government systems.

Recognizing Cyber-security

Cyber-security steps are set up because almost any Information stored on a personal computer or electronic apparatus or over the Web can be retrieved, and also with the correct measures in place, this may be prevented.

Inorder to Make Sure That a machine is protected, an Individual needs to Understand the dangers and vulnerabilities inherent to this particular apparatus or system and whether these vulnerabilities are exploitable.

Key take aways

- cyber-security could be your measures taken to guard electronic advice.
- Cyber-security can help keep identity thieves from hacking computers or digital apparatus.
- Password security and disc encryption are all types of cyber-security measures.

Sorts of Cyber-attacks

Hazards to your pc program are classified by the procedure Used to assault. When there are lots of kinds of cyber-attacks, a number of the very frequent types include these:

- back-door strikes use any alternative ways of obtaining something which do not require the typical procedures of authentication. Many systems include such back-doors by-design, but some lead to one.
- Denial of service strikes forbid the rightful user from accessing this system. A frequent process of the sort of cyber-attack is entering a wrong password repeatedly which the account is secured.
- Direct access strikes include viruses and bugs, that get access to some platform and copy its own information or alter the technique.
- Cases of Cyber-security Measures
- Cyber-security ranges from easy to complex. As a fundamental Preventative step, many devices have been equipped with password security to stop hacking. When a machine is assaulted or in the an increased risk of an attack, then specific measures may be studied with regards to the sort of attack. By way of instance, disk is 1 method to stop direct access strikes.

So as to Work, Cyber-security steps Must always adapt to new technologies and improvements. Hackers accommodate their solutions to fresh kinds of cyber-security and leave it inefficient, or so the security apps must stay 1 step ahead.

Shared Targets of Cyber-attacks

While any person system reaches any degree of Cyberattack hazard, larger entities such as government and business systems tend to be the targets of those strikes. The Department of Homeland Security uses high tech cyber-security measures to protect sensitive government information from various other nations, nation-states, and hackers.

Any fiscal system which stores charge card Info From its customers reaches a risky since hackers could steal money from those by obtaining these reports. Huge organizations are usually assaulted, since they store personal advice regarding their large network of employees. Other goals include systems which control infrastructures, like telecommunications and energy systems, since individuals try to restrain this particular equipment.

Common Kinds of Cyber-security Attacks

In a Glance:

Should you have Ever researched famous conflicts ever, you will recognize that no 2 will be exactly alike. Still, you will find definite plans and approaches usually utilized in conflict since they're time-proven to work.

Similarly, If an offender is seeking to hack on organization, they won't re invent the wheel till they have to: They will draw up on ordinary kinds of hacking methods which can be understood to be extremely effective, such as malware, phishing, or even cross-site scripting (XSS). Whether you are attempting to make awareness of the hottest data breach mantra from the news headlines or assessing a incident on your organization, it will help to comprehend different attack vectors a malicious celebrity may possibly attempt to cause injury. Here is an summary of a number of the very typical kinds of attacks found now.

Malware

Should you have Ever noticed an antivirus alarm popup in your monitor, or when you have wrongly clicked on a malicious email attachment, and then you've experienced a close call with malware. Attackers want to utilize malware to acquire a foothold in users' computers and, thus, the offices that they work in -- since it might be so powerful.

"Malware" Identifies several kinds of harmful applications, like viruses and ransom-ware. Once malware remains on your pc, it might wreak all kinds of havoc, by taking charge of one's own machine, to tracking your own activities and keystrokes, to quietly sending a variety of confidential data out of the pc or system into the attacker's home base.

Attackers Can make use of a number of ways to access malware in your pc, however in any point often it takes an individual to have a method to put in malware. This may consist of clicking a URL to download a document, or establishing an attachment which can appear harmless (just like a Word file or PDF attachment), but has an malware hidden within.

Phishing

Of Course, odds are you'll not simply open a random attachment or click a link in any email which comes your way there needs become a compelling basis that you do it. Attackers understand that, too. As soon as an attacker would like one to install malware or disclose sensitive data, they usually turn into phishing approaches, or pretending to be somebody else or something different for one to choose a task you ordinarily would not. As they count on individual fascination and instincts, phishing attacks might be hard to prevent.

At a Phishing attack an individual can send you a email which seems to be from somebody that you trust, such as your boss or perhaps a company that you work with. The email will appear logical, and it'll have a urgency for this (e.g. fraudulent activity was discovered in your own accounts). From the mail, there'll undoubtedly be an attachment to either start or perhaps a hyperlink to see. Upon launching the malicious attachment, then you will hence install malware from your PC. If you follow on the connection, it can send one to some legitimate-looking site which asks that you sign into to get into an crucial document --but that the site is really a snare used to catch your credentials when you attempt to sign into.

Inorder To battle phishing efforts, understanding the significance of confirming email senders and also attachments/links is vital.

SQL Injection Attack

SQL (pronounced "sequel") represents structured query language; it is really a programming language used to communicate with all databases. A number of the servers which store significant data for services and websites utilize SQL to deal with the data within their databases. A SQL injection attack expressly targets this type of host, using malicious code to have the host to disclose information it ordinarily would not. That is particularly problematic in the event the host stores confidential purchaser information from the site, such as credit card numbers, user names and passwords (certificate), or other personally identifiable details, that can be lucrative and tempting goals for a attacker.

An SQL Injection attack operates by exploiting any of those famous SQL vulnerabilities that permit the SQL server to perform malicious code. By way of instance, if your SQL server is exposed to a injection attack, it might be easy for an individual to visit a site's search box and key in code which could induce your website's SQL host to ditch most its stored user names and passwords to the website.

Cross-Site Scripting (XSS)

In a SQL Injection attackan attacker moves after having a exposed internet site to a target its stored data, such as user credentials or sensitive financial data. However, when the attacker could preferably instantly aim an internet site's customers, then they can elect to get a cross-site scripting attack. Much like an SQL injection attack, this attack additionally involves putting malicious code to your site, in this event the internet site it self is never being assaulted. As an alternative, the malicious code that the attacker has recovered just rans from the consumer's browser whenever they see the assaulted internet site, also it moves after visitors right, and not the site.

Certainly one of The most typical ways an attacker may set up a cross-site scripting attack would be by injecting malicious code into an opinion or even a script which may mechanically ran. By way of instance, they can embed a URL to some malicious Java Script at a comment on the site.

Cross-site Scripting strikes may substantially harm a site's standing by setting the users' information at an increased risk with no sign that whatever malicious actually occurred. Any sensitive information that a user sends into your website --such as with their identity, credit card info, or any other confidential data--could be retrieved via cross-site scripting minus the website owners recognizing that there is a problem at the first location.

Denial of service (DoS)

Imagine You are sitting on a one-lane country road, with cars backed up so much as the eye could see. Ordinarily this road sees over an automobile or 2, however a county fair and also a leading sporting event have stopped across exactly the exact same period, also this road could be the sole means for individuals to leave town. The trail can not deal with the huge level of traffic, so that consequently it becomes really copied that pretty much no you may render.

That is Essentially what goes on to a internet site in a denial of service (DoS) attack. In the event that you flood a website with more traffic than it had been constructed to take care of, you'll overload the site's server and it's going be more nigh-impossible for your own site to function up its articles to people that are attempting to get it.

This really is Happen for benign reasons needless to say, state should a gigantic news narrative breaks along with also a paper's internet site becomes bombarded with traffic from those attempting to discover more. But this type of traffic overload is malicious, even as a attacker flooding a site by having a overwhelming quantity of traffic to essentially shut down it to users.

In certain Examples, these DoS attacks have been performed by lots of computers at precisely the exact same moment. The scenario of attack will be called a Distributed denial of service Attack (DDoS). This form of attack might be more challenging to overcome as a result of attacker arising out of numerous IP addresses across the globe simultaneously, which makes determining the foundation of the attack a lot harder for system administrators.

Session Hijacking and also Man in the Middle Attacks

When You are on the World-wide web, your computer has a great deal of small back and forth trades with servers across the globe enabling them understand that who you are and asking specific sites or solutions. But in exchange, if all goes as it should, the servers should answer your petition giving you the information you are getting. This technique, or session, happens if you're simply browsing or whenever you're logging to a website with your password and username.

The Session between the pc and the remote server is provided a exceptional session ID, which ought to stay confidential between both parties; nevertheless, an attacker may hijack the session by getting the SESSIONID and posing since the computer implementing, letting them sign into within a unsuspecting user and access bogus information online server. There are quite a few ways an attacker could use to sneak the session ID, like a cross-site scripting attack utilized to pierce session IDs.

An Attacker may also decide to ditch the session to fit themselves between the asking computer and the remote server, even pretending to become one other party inside the semester. This makes it possible for them to intercept information from both directions and is often known as a Man in the Middle attack.

Credential Re-Use

Users Now have many logins and passwords to bear in mind it is tempting to reuse credentials there or here to make life somewhat simpler. Though security practices recommend you have unique passwords for most of your websites and applications, a lot of folks still reuse their passwords well known fact attackers rely upon.

Once Investors possess a selection of user names and passwords out of the busted internet site or service (readily acquired on almost any range of black-market internet sites online)they understand that should they utilize these exact credentials on different internet sites there is an opportunity they will have the ability to sign into. However tempting it could be to recreate credentials for the email, banking accounts, as well as your favorite sports discussion, it is likely that a single day that the discussion will probably get hacked, even giving an attacker easy access for a bank and email accounts. In regards to credentials, number is indispensable. Password managers can be obtained and will be helpful in regards to managing the several credentials you're using.

That really is Only a choice of common attack types and methods. It isn't designed to be methodical, and attackers will develop and develop new techniques as needed; nevertheless, being mindful of, and these sorts of strikes will considerably enhance your security position.

Hacker's Role in Cyber-security

World-wide earnings loss because of malicious hackers yearly Reaches figures from the centuries. To combat this increasing threat, employers, institutes of higher education, and government agencies are working diligently to organize another generation of cyber-security experts. These professionals will probably soon be adept at identifying, isolating, and reacting appropriately to risks as promptly as possible to be able to efficiently minimize damage.

Ethical Hacking Training

In order to completely assess a system's safety, it's Necessary to go through the complete extent of this vulnerabilities. This is really where trained ethical hackers return into mimic the processes of an intruder, however with the goal of solving the security dilemma rather than exploiting it to get doubtful advantage. Ethical hackers are trustworthy and also have honed their wisdom and ability under moral process. They normally operate in an extremely secured environment in a office setting, but their hours in many cases are un-traditional, as an offender hacker hours will generally be. The ethical hacker tracks the networks in various times and degrees of activity to assess threat levels which may exist in non-peak usage intervals.

With powerful programming and media understanding, they Perform system audits to get numerous kinds of data that's subsequently utilized to exhibit a general picture of an whole company's cyber-related security challenges. As a result of the highly technical skillset they possess, and also the extreme relevance of the essence of these job, they're on average highly admired for their devotion to preventing cyberattacks.

Most moral hackers possess extensive on the job coaching and Exceptionally intricate comprehension of how network security is assembled. They will need to be meticulous and patient within their procedures and thorough in their recordkeeping. Exotic hackers stay sought after in all businesses all over the worldwide market place.

Legal Risks

Ethical hackers need to complete a rigorous set of desktop Tests included in their hiring process, as organizations normally don't hire ex-hackers using a prohibited ago. Licensed hackers are an self-policing staff who discuss best practice solutions to promote favorable outcomes. Additionally, various professional classes can additionally promote codes of behavior to decide on a standard of professional behavior. As an example, the Association of Information Technology Professionals lays on a code of behavior that underscores the significance of ethical and legally-binding treatment of most information that's viewed throughout ethical hacking circumstances.

Intense legal implications exist for hackers who Stray from ethical methods or ignore privacy arrangements. Still, there are always legal risks if exposing vulnerabilities with regularly significant bets, therefore the field all together has to continue to react to legal concerns since it continues to evolve.

Certification Apps

For professionals considering cyber-security, innovative coursework will demand some Amount of ethical hacking. As certificate and degree programs carry on to react to industry demand for skilled cyber-security experts, caregivers using the technical and social skills to comprehend and also minimize the danger of cyberattacks possess several alternatives for continuing their education and increasing their own knowledge base.

Top-tier and regionally accredited applications demand Simulations that prepare the future generation of cyber-security pros to recognize early indicators of a potential hazard or attack across many different platforms. Trained in ethical hacking involves handling common concerns, including employee password along with notebook theft, in addition to some other dangers including outside malicious attacks from professional hacking associations, internal security breaches because of employee fraud or even sometimes ignorance, along with hardware limits which may cause greater exposure. A few cyber-security professionals work to deal with corporate culture problems like employee training on special security-related troubles.

Turning Suggestions to a Trade

With increasing global requirement for highly proficient Professional cyber-security experts, internship will last to be much more strict. Some of the vital facets to combat malicious hacking would be that the corporate utilization of hackers to find and strengthen weak stains until prohibited hackers find and harness them.

Though successful, ethical hacking isn't without its challenges. Cyber-security professionals now seeking applicable training ought to carefully take into consideration the reach of training and breadth of technical wisdom readily available in future coaching programs. With the greater requirement and global opportunity, professionals trying to progress within the area of cyber-security do have significantly more options and regions of specialization readily available for them than previously.

CHAPTER THREE
FUNDAMENTALS OF HACKING

What Exactly Is Hacktivism?

Hacktivism Is a political or social activist act that's performed by breaking to and wreaking havoc on a safe computer program. Hacktivism is normally directed in government or corporate goals. The groups or people which take out hacktivism are also known as hacktivists.

Hacktivists' Goals incorporate religious associations, terrorists, drug dealers, and pedophiles. A good instance of hacktivism is currently refusal of service strikes (DoS) which closed a system to stop customer access. Other instances involve providing citizens using government-censored web-pages or providing privacy-protected way of communicating to endangered classes (such as Syrians through the Arab Spring).

Hacktivism Is a mixture of"hacking" and"activism" and will be claimed to have already been chased by the hacktivist group Cult of the Dead Cow (CdC).

Key Take-Aways

- Hacktivism involves breaking into a computer system and making changes which influence a individual or organization.

- Targets vary between religious businesses to drug dealers and pedophiles.

- Many activists utilize hacktivism and on-site protesting. Examples comprise Occupy WallStreet and the Church of Scientology protests.

The Way Hacktivism Works

Hacktivism's Aims include these:

- Circumventing government censorship by helping taxpayers get to domestic firewalls or helping protestors to prepare on the web

- utilizing social media marketing platforms to market human rights or help censored taxpayers of oppressive regimes speak with   the surface world

- shooting down administration internet sites which pose a threat to active taxpayers

- Protecting free language on the web

- Promoting usage of information

- Donating citizen uprisings

- Assisting computer users at protecting their own privacy   and   avoiding   surveillance   through anonymous and secure networks like Tor and the Reminders messaging program

- Disrupting corporate or corporate power
- helps illegal immigrants cross boundaries firmly
- Donating democracy
- Protesting exemptions and globalization
- Protesting acts of warfare
- Halting the backing of terrorism.
- Hacktivists' Techniques might comprise distributed denial of service (DDoS) attacks, which flood a site or email address using this much traffic it melts down; data theft; internet site defacement; viruses and viruses which disperse protest messages; carrying social networking reports, and stealing and revealing sensitive data.

There Was Debate over the hacktivist community through which methods are appropriate and that aren't. By way of instance, while hacktivists may possibly assert encouraging free language being a major reason, using DoS attacks, internet site defacements, and data theft which hinder or keep free language might be at odds with this objective. The techniques hacktivists utilize are prohibited and so are an application of cyber-crime. Yet they oftentimes aren't prosecuted as they're rarely investigated by police force. It could be hard for police to spot both the hackers and damages which ensure often be modest.

Hacktivism Can be applied as a replacement for or complement to conventional kinds of activism such as for example sites and demonstration marches. It has happened with all the Occupy Wall Street and Church of Scientology protests, which included the physical presence of fans from the roads and internet strikes. Hacktivist strikes themselves aren't abusive and do not put protestors in danger of physical injury, unlike engaging in a street demonstration, however in some cases, hacktivism may wreak havoc. Hacktivism additionally makes it feasible to encourage distant causes and never being forced to visit there and also allows geographically dispersed individuals who have shared goals to combine and act in service of a shared objective.

Cases of Hacktivism

Even though That there are hundreds and hundreds of hacktivist collections worldwide, a number of those overburdened out of the 1990s to the present day comprise CdC, Hacktivismo, Lulz Security (Lulz Sec), Anonymous, Legions of the Underground, The Electronic Disturbance

Theater, Young Intelligent Hackers Against Terrorism, Syrian Electronics Army, along with AnonGhost.

Ethical Hacking Basics (E|HF) can be a entry-level security tool since the fundamental concepts of information security. It equips students with the skills essential to spot the rising information security dangers which think on the security position of their company and also execute general security controllers.

This App provides holistic summary of the vital aspects of information security. It supplies a reliable fundamental knowledge needed for a career in information security.

The E|HF Is made for all those considering learning the many principles of information security.

Why E|HF Is Very Important

- It eases your entry into the world of data security
- It Offers an Expert Comprehension of this Theories of information security
- It provides best methods to enhance Organizational safety position
- It enriches your abilities like a Security Specialist and raises your own employability

What's Your Dark Net?

The "dark web" and "darkened net" connote A sub set of secret sites which you can get within a encrypted network.

Although the net dominates every aspect of the Daily lives in the moment, it is vital to bear in mind it has just existed for a couple decades. While that can be a rather brief length of time in comparison to the program of history, it's a large number of technological lifetimes. Therefore, the web is a exceptionally amazing location, a period of countless different websites which can be associated with another in an elaborate blend of means.

Even the Most Well-known Sites, such as Facebook (FB), Google (GOOG) and Amazon (AMZN) are all well-known across the environment. Besides those preferred websites, there's a far bigger assortment of less traveled pieces of the World-wide web. And lurking beyond each one the basic, accessible regions of the internet are different pockets of internet sites. These past groups constitute the socalled "black net" or even "dark web."

'Dark Net' Versus 'Deep Web'

The phrases "dark web" and also "darknet" are Sporadically used interchangeably but with subtle differences in significance. They generally connote a sub set of sites that exist within a system that's encrypted.

That the system is encrypted signifies that it Isn't Searchable by conventional methods, like an internet search engine, also it's really perhaps not observable through conventional browsers. Dark baits exist in many shapes, and also the definition of itself will not necessarily imply any nefarious undertones. A black net is any overlay system that demands special consent or applications to get.

Why would individuals want to sponsor websites on a black net? Dark baits are generally related to a number of distinct purposes. They are sometimes used for lots of crimes, including illegal filesharing, black markets, as well as a way for the market of prohibited services or goods. All these are frequently the most highly-publicized applications of a dark website.

However, they're also employed for a bunch of different explanations. Dark Nets tend to be contacted as a way of protecting political dissidents out of reprisal, or even as something for allowing people to bypass censorship networks. They are able to ease whistle-blowing and news flows, plus so they are able to help protect individuals from surveillance. Therefore, and as a consequence of the great number of software of a black net, they're a hotly contested issue.

"Dark internet" is frequently mistaken with "profound web." The profound web identifies un-indexed websites that are unsearchable; in the majority of instances, this can be only because the internet sites are protected with passwords. "Dark net" websites are intentionally hidden from the outside net by additional ways. A massive most online websites constitute the "deep web," while they truly are password-protected.

Encryption as well as also the Dark Net

Some of the common methods that dark baits are split out From the outside net is by way of encryption. Most shadowy sites make use of the Tor encryption tool that will help hide their individuality.

Tor Permits People to conceal their place, appearing as If they're in another nation. Tor-encrypted systems require which individuals use Tor so as to see them. Ergo, all those users' IP addresses along with other identifying information will be encrypted. Most this combines to imply that many people can see websites on the darkened net, as long because they will have the right security tools.

However, it might be unbelievably tough to establish who oversees the internet sites. Additionally, it suggests that, if anybody engaging from the darkened net gets her or his identity disclosed, it may be dangerous.

Tor uses layers and layers of protection, procuring Traffic by turning it via a compact system of secure relays to anonymize it. Tor isn't prohibited applications in and of it self, at precisely the exact same fashion that torrenting programs aren't prohibited. (See too: Just How Can Bit Torrent Websites Much like The Pirate Bay Generate Income?) In either instances, however, the computer software is often utilized to ran prohibited actions (either via the darkened net or, even in the instance of all torrenting applications, to download (substance).

To place Tor's dark web connections in context, It's useful to Bear in mind that Tor quotes just about 4 percent of its traffic is still useful for darknet Services, together with the remaining simply accounted for by folks obtaining Normal sites by having an higher amount of anonymity and security.

Infamous Cases of This Dark Net

When most Men and Women think about this dark web, Several notable Examples spring to mind. All these are networks or sites of websites which are made headlines for just one reason or the other. Many are prohibited for a couple of reasons. But, you can find additional potential black baits, and never most them are fundamentally prohibited.

Certainly one of the Most Well-known examples of a darkened community has been that the Silk Road market. Silk Road has been a internet site used for your buying and sale of many different prohibited items, for example recreational weapons and drugs.

Silk Road was set in 2011 and is frequently considered the very first black net sector. Even though it was closed down from authorities in 2013, it's spawned quite a few copy cat markets.

Market Places like Silk Road were instrumental from the Development of crypto currencies, the majority that rely upon decentralization and improved security measures. The solitude and anonymity of several crypto currencies has got them the possibility of preference when completing trades in shadowy markets.

Reasons to Use or Avoid The Dark Web

Besides prohibited purchases and earnings, you can find Legitimate reasons you may be enthusiastic about using the shadowy website. Individuals within closed societies and confronting extreme censorship may utilize darknet to interact with others beyond society. Even folks in open societies may possibly have some fascination with utilizing the shadowy net, specially as concerns regarding government snooping and data collection continue to rise worldwide.

Yet, a large Part of the action that takes Put on the darkened net is prohibited. It isn't tricky to surmise this could be the case: that the darkened net supplies a degree of individuality security which the top net will not. Criminals appearing to secure their identities as a way to prevent detection and catch are attracted for the facet of the dark website. Because of this, it's unsurprising that numerous noteworthy hacks and statistics breaches are linked to the darknet in a roundabout manner or another.

In 2015, as an Example, a trove of consumer info had been Stolen from Ashley Madison, an internet site purporting to offer partners a way of cheating in their spouses. The stolen data revealed upon the shadowy net, where it was later recovered and distributed to the general public. Back in 20-16, then-U.S. attorney-general Loretta Lynch cautioned that gun sales happening across the shadowy net have become more prevalent, since it enabled sellers and buyers to prevent regulations. Illegal pornography is just another relatively common phenomenon on the shadowy net.

Contemplating the nefarious underbelly of this shadowy web, it is No real surprise that a lot of folks don't have any reason to get it. And given the higher significance of crypto currencies in the planet, it's likely that shadowy nets will get more of an attribute for ordinary internet users later on. Meanwhile they may possibly also still provide offenders a way of eluding catch, even though true anonymity is not fully guaranteed, even if utilizing encryption of this type seen in those programs.

Phishing attacks

What's a phishing attack
Phishing Is a Kind of social engineering assault frequently Employed To steal consumer data, including login

credentials and bank card numbers. It occurs when an attacker, even uttered as a trusted thing, dupes a victim to opening a message, instant message text or text. The receiver is then duped into clicking a malicious connection, which may cause the setup of malware, even the freezing of this machine as a portion of a ransom-ware attack or perhaps the showing of sensitive details.

An attack could have catastrophic outcomes. For people, This comprises unauthorized purchases, the slumping of capital, or spot theft.

Additionally, infantry is often Utilized to gain a foothold in Governmental or corporate systems as part of a bigger attack, like an advanced level persistent hazard (APT) event. In this scenario, employees are endangered as a way to circumvent security perimeters, disperse malware in a closed atmosphere, or gain automatic access to data that is secured.

A company sentenced to this assault generally Sustains severe financial losses as well as decreasing market share, standing, and consumer confidence. Based on extent, a phishing effort may possibly escalate to some security episode from that a business is going to have a tricky time recovering.

Phishing Methods

Email Encryption scams

Email is really a statistics game. An attacker sending outside Tens of thousands of deceptive messages may net substantial info and amounts of money, even when just a tiny fraction of recipients fall for your scam. As mentioned previously, you can find a few methods people use to raise their success prices.

For starters, they ll go to amazing lengths in designing Phishing messages to mimic actual emails from the spoofed company. Employing exactly the very same phrasing, typefaces, logos, and signatures which makes the messages appear plausible.

Additionally, attackers will usually attempt to drive customers Actions by making a feeling of immediacy. By way of instance, as previously shown, an email may sabotage accounts expiration and set the receiver on a timer. Applying such pressure induces the consumer to be diligent and much more prone to mistake.

Last, links within messages resemble their valid Presents, however, normally possess a domain or extra sub domains. From the above mentioned case, the myuniversity.edu/renewal URL had been shifted to myuniversity.edurenewal.com. Similarities between both addresses supply the belief of a secure connection, which makes the receiver more conscious that the attack is happening.

Spear-phishing

Spear Phishing aims a particular individual or enterprise, instead of arbitrary application consumers. It's really a in-depth model of phishing which necessitates special understanding about a company, for example its power architecture.

An assault Could perform the following:

- A perpetrator investigates titles of employees within a business's marketing department and benefits access to the most recent job statements.
- Posing whilst the advertising manager, the attacker mails a departmental manager (PM) with a subject line which reads," Upgraded invoice for Q 3 campaigns. The written text, style, also contained logo duplicate the company's standard email template.

- A connection inside the email results in some password-protected internal record, that is actually a spoofed version of a encoded statement.
- The PM is asked to loginto to view the document. The attacker accomplishes his credentials, acquiring complete access to sensitive areas within the company's network.
- By Providing an individual with valid login credentials, spear-phishing is a fruitful way of implementing the very first period of an APT.

The way to Reduce phishing

Phishing Attack coverage requires measures be obtained by both the enterprises and users.

To get Users, vigilance is essential. A spoofed message frequently contains subtle mistakes which expose its identity. These may incorporate spelling mistakes or changes on domain names, as seen at the prior URL example. Users must stop and think of the reason why they truly are also receiving this kind of email address.

To get Enterprises, several steps might be used to reevaluate both the phishing and spear phishing attacks:

- Two-factor authentication (2FA) has become easily the best way of countering malware attacks, even as it includes an excess confirmation coating when logging into to sensitive software. 2FA is based on users using two things: something that they understand, like a password and username, and something that they will have, like their tablets. Even if employees are jeopardized, 2FA averts using these endangered credentials, since these are not enough to acquire entrance.

- As well as using 2FA, businesses should apply strict password management policies. By way of instance, employees must be asked to usually alter their passwords and also not be allowed to reuse a password for several software.

- Educational campaigns may also help decrease the chance of phishing attacks by applying protected techniques, for example rather than clicking external email links.

- Phishing protection against Imperva

Imperva Supplies a mixture of access control and web application security methods to cancel malicious efforts:

- Imperva login Shield permits you to deploy 2FA security for URL addresses from your site or web application. This comprises addresses using URL parameters or AJAX pages, at which 2FA security is normally tougher to implement. The answer may be set in minutes with only a couple clicks of mouse. It will not require any software or hardware setup and enables easy control of user functions and rights directly out of the Imperva dashboard.

- Working inside the cloud, Imperva Web Application Firewall (WAF) cubes malicious asks at the edge of your own network. This consists of preventing malware attempts by endangered insiders furthermore to represented XSS strikes deriving from the malware episode.

- What is Malware? The Way Malware Works & How To Eliminate It

- The Expression malware is really a Regeneration of malicious tender ware. To put it differently, malware isn't any piece of computer software which has been written with the goal of harmful apparatus, concealing data, and generally resulting in a wreck. Viruses, Trojans, spyware, and even ransom-ware are just one of the different forms of malware.

Malware is frequently Produced by groups of hackers: generally, They truly are only attempting to earn money, by simply dispersing the malware or attempting to sell it to the maximum bidder on the dark Internet. But, there may be additional good reasons for creating malware it might be applied as something for demonstration, a means to check security, and on occasion whilst weapons of warfare between authorities.

But Regardless of why or malware has been, it is consistently Poor news if it pops through to your own PC. As luck would have it, that is what we're here to avert.

Exactly what exactly does malware?

All types Of matters. It's really a really wide category, and also what malware does or malware works varies from document. This is a set of common kinds of malware, however it's scarcely methodical:

- Virus: Similar to the biological namesakes viruses connect to wash files and also preempt additional files that are clean. They are able to spread buoyant, damaging something's core functionality and copying or deleting files. They generally appear like a executable file (.exe).
- Trojans: This sort of malware disguises itself as valid applications, or has been hidden in valid applications that's been tampered with. It is inclined

to behave discreetly and make back doors on your security to allow additional malware.

- Spy-ware: no real surprise -- spyware is malware built to spy you. It hides in the background and also takes notes about which you can do online, as well as your passwords, credit card numbers, surfing customs, and much more.

- Worms: Worms infect entire networks of apparatus, either across the World-wide web, using network ports. It employs each and every infected system to infect the others.

- Ransom-ware: This sort of malware an average of protects your computer along with your own files, and compromises to erase all if you don't buy a ransom.

- Ad-ware: Though maybe not necessarily malicious in nature, competitive advertising applications could endanger your security merely to last adverts -- that could provide additional malware a simple way in. Plus, let us face it pop-ups are very annoying.

- Bot-nets: Botnets are networks of infected computers which can be made to interact under the hands of the attacker.

- The best way to shield against malware

- In regards to pollution, avoidance is much far better than a cure. Luckily, you can find a number of frequent sense, easy behaviors which minimize your odds of ranning into some other nasty applications.

- Do not expect strangers online! "Social engineering", that can consist of strange emails, unexpected alarms, bogus profiles, and also curiosity-tickling provides, and would be the number 1 way of sending malware. If you never know just what it really is, do not click onto it.

- Doublecheck your own downloads! By pirating internet sites to official store-fronts, malware can be lurking around the corner. Before downloading, always double-check that the provider is trusted by attentively reading reviews and opinions.

- Receive an Adblocker! Malvertising -- by which hackers utilize infected banner ads or popup adverts to infect your apparatus -- is still on the upswing. You can not understand that adverts are awful: therefore that it's safer to block all of them with a trusted Adblocker.

- Figuring out at which you navigate! Malware are available anywhere, however it's most typical in websites with inferior back end security, such as small, local sites. If you stay glued to high, reputable websites, you badly lower your chance of breaking malware.

The best way to discover malware

Certain breeds of malware are easier to find than The others. Some, such as ransom-ware and spyware, create their presence known instantly, by simply assessing your files or simply by streaming unlimited advertisements at you. The others, such as Trojans and spyware, venture out of the way to cover up from you so long as feasible, meaning that they are in your own system quite a very long time until you recognize they're present. And there are many others, such as worms and viruses, which may operate in secret for some moment, until the signs of these illness start to seem, such as icy, deleted or substituted files, abrupt shutdowns, or perhaps a hyperactive process or.

The only surefire way to discover all of malware before it Infects your computer, Mac, or phone will be to put in anti-virus applications, that can come packed with detection scans and tools which may capture malware now in your own apparatus, in addition to block malware hoping to infect it.

How to remove malware

Each Kind of malware has got its way of infecting and Damaging data and computers, and thus each requires an alternative malware removal approach. To begin, have a look at our hints for eliminating malware and viruses.

Nevertheless, the best way to Remain secure or eliminate an Illness is touse anti-virus applications, additionally referred to as antivirus. The ideal malware removal software are comprised from the most advanced level anti-virus, and sometimes even free ones such as AVG antivirus FREE possess all you want to remain safe from probably the most typical dangers.

What is Hacking?

Hacking is identifying weaknesses in pc programs Or programs to exploit its flaws to obtain access. Example of Pairing: Utilizing password partitioning algorithm to Access your Method

Computers have become compulsory to operate a powerful Companies. It's insufficient to possess remote computers systems; however they ought to get networked to ease communication with outside companies. It exposes them into the exterior world and also hacking. Pairing means using computers to commit deceptive acts like fraud, privacy intrusion, stealing corporate/personal data, etc.. Cybercrimes cost many companies tens of thousands of dollars per year. Organizations will need to safeguard themselves against such strikes.

What's cyber-crime?

Cybercrime is that the usage of networks and computers to do Prohibited activities like spreading computer viruses, online bullying, performing unauthorized electronic fund transfers, etc.. Many cyber-crimes are committed via the World-wide web. A few cyber-crimes may be completed with Mobile mobiles via SMS and internet booting software.

Form of Cyber-crime

- These list presents the normal kinds of cyber-crimes:
- Pc Fraud: Intentional deception for personal profit via using pcs.
- Privacy breach: Exposing personal info like email addresses, phone number, account details, etc.. On interpersonal networking, sites, etc..
- Identity-theft: Stealing personal advice from some body and respecting this person.
- Sharing copyrighted files/information: This involves dispersing copyright protected files such as eBooks and computer apps etc..

- Electronic funds transfer: this calls for obtaining an unauthorized accessibility to bank networks along with manufacturing illegal fund transfers.

- Electronic cash laundering: This also involves Using this pc to make cash.

- ATM Fraud: this calls for intercepting ATM card details like telephone number and PIN numbers. These records are then utilized to draw funds out of the secured accounts.

- Denial of Service Attacks: This also entails using computers in numerous locations to attack hosts with a perspective of shutting down them.

- Spam: Sending deceptive emails. These emails usually feature adverts.

What's Ethical Hacking?

Ethical Hacking is pinpointing weakness in pcs or computer networks and forthcoming together with counter measures that protect the flaws. Ethical hackers must comply by these rules.

Obtain written consent by the person who owns the laptop system or pc system prior hacking on.

Protect the solitude of this company been murdered.

Transparently report all of the identified flaws inside the computer approach into your company.

Why Ethical Hacking?

Info is among the very valuable assets of a organization. Maintaining information safe can protect a business's image and save a business plenty of funds.

Hacking may cause lack of company for associations which deal in fund such as pay pal. Ethical hacking sets them a step in front of those cyber offenders who'd otherwise contribute to lack in business.

Legality of Ethical Hacking

Ethical Hacking is legal in case the consumer abides by the rules stipulated in the above mentioned section on this is of hacking. The International Council of all e-commerce Consultants (ec council) supplies a certificate program that assesses patient's skills. People that pass the exam have been given using certificates. The certifications should be revived after a moment.

Overview

- Hacking is both exploiting and identifying flaws in pcs and/or computer systems.

- Cyber-crime is committing a crime with the assistance of computers and information technology infrastructure.
- Ethical Hacking is all about improving the security of pcs and/or computer systems.
- Ethical Hacking isn't legal.

Possible Security Risks To Your Personal Computer Systems

A pc system hazard is something which contributes to Loss or corruption of data or bodily harm to the infrastructure or hardware. Focusing on just how to determine computer security dangers maybe your initial action in protecting pcs. The dangers can possibly be deliberate, unintentional or due to natural disasters.

In this Report, We'll present you to the shared Computer system dangers and the way it is possible to protect systems.

Security Threat is described as a threat what may Potentially damage personal computers as well as company. The reason might possibly be physical like somebody stealing a computer which has data that is essential. The reason might also be non physical such because of being a virus attack. In such tutorial show, we'll specify a hazard as a possible attack in the hacker which may permit them to get unauthorized use of a laptop strategy.

Which are Physical Risks?

A bodily danger is a Possible reason for the Incident which might lead to loss or bodily damage to your pcs.

This list classifies the bodily dangers into Three (3) main categories;

- Inner: The dangers involve fire, shaky power source, humidity at the chambers home the equipment, etc..
- Topical: All these dangers incorporate Lightning, flooding and earthquakes, etc..
- Individual: All these dangers include vandalism, theft of the infrastructure or hardware, disturbance, accidental or deliberate mistakes.

This list shows a number of the Probable steps that Could be obtained:

- Inner: Fire risks might possibly be prevented by using automatic fire detectors and extinguishers which don't use water to create a flame pit. The shaky power source might be prevented by using voltage controls. An air conditioner may be employed to manage the humidity from the living space.

- Topical: Lightning security systems may be used to protect personal computers against such strikes. Lightning protection systems aren't 100 percent perfect, however to a certain degree, they also reduce the odds of Lightning inducing damage. Housing personal computers in high-tech are among the probable means of protecting systems against flooding.
- People: Threats like theft might be prevented using doors that are locked and limited accessibility to personal rooms.

Which are nonphysical dangers?

A Nonphysical hazard is a Possible reason for the Incident which might come in;

- corruption or reduction of system data
- Disrupt industry operations which rely on pcs
- loss in sensitive information
- Illegal observation of tasks on pcs

Cyber-security Breaches

the others

The Nonphysical dangers can also be Called plausible threats. This listing is your most popular Kinds of Non Physical dangers;

- Virus
- Trojans
- Worms
- Spy-ware
- Key loggers
- Ad-ware
- Denial of Service Attacks
- Distributed Denial of Service Attacks
- Unauthorized Use of Pcs tools including information
- Phishing

Additional Computer Security Risks

To safeguard computer programs from the Above-mentioned dangers, a business should possess legitimate security measures inplace. This list shows a number of the Probable steps Which Can Be required to safeguard cyber safety dangers

To Safeguard against viruses, Trojans, worms, etc.. Company may use anti-virus applications . In addition to this anti-virus applications, a business also can provide control measures to the using outside storage apparatus as well as visiting the site that's quite prone to down load bogus apps on the consumer's computer.

Unauthorized entry to computer system tools Could be avoided by using authentication techniques. Even the authentication techniques could be, also in the kind of user ids and strong passwords, smart cards or biometric, etc..

Intrusion-detection/prevention systems may be utilized To shield against denial of service attacks. You will find different measures too which will be set in position to prevent denial of service attacks.

Overview

- A hazard isn't any activity which could cause data loss/corruption right through to disturbance of normal business operations.
- You will find physical and nonphysical threats
- Physical dangers cause injury to computer systems infrastructure and hardware. Cases include vandalism, theft right through to natural disasters.
- Nonphysical risks aim the data and software on the pc systems.
- Thinking about know to app?

- Hackers would be the problem solver and application builders, learning how to schedule can assist you to implement solutions to issues. Additionally, it distinguishes you from script kids.

- Composing programs as being a newbie can allow you automate many tasks that may ordinarily require a lot of time and energy to finish.

- Composing programs may also allow you to identify and then use programming errors in software you will probably be targeting.

- You never need to re-invent the wheel all of the time, also you can find a range of open source apps which are easily usable. You are able to customize the existing software and also add your techniques to fit your preferences.

What languages should I know?

The Reply to the query Is Dependent upon Your Goal Computer platforms and systems. Some programming languages have been used to grow for just specific platforms. For example, VisualBasic Classic (4, 3, 5, and 6.0) can be applied to publish software that ran using Windows os. It might, consequently, be illogical that you find out to program from Visual Basic 6.0 if your target will be hacking on Linux established systems.

CHAPTER FOUR
END USERS, ACCOUNTS AND
PASSWORDS MANAGEMENT

In the event that you thought passwords will undoubtedly be dead, then reconsider. They truly are here to stay -- for today. Passwords are awkward and difficult to consider -- and only when you did, you are told to improve it out. And passwords may be figured and can easily be hackable.

Nobody enjoys passwords however they are a simple fact of life. Along with While others have tried to kill off them by substituting them with fingerprints and also face-scanning technology, neither are perfect and most still hotel back into the convenient (but bothersome) password.

Just how do you create sure they are better? You require a password manager.

What's a password manager?
Think about a password supervisor just like a publication of your passwords, Secured by means of a master secret that you realize.

A number of you feel that may seem awful. Imagine if somebody Gets my password? That is clearly an honest and logical fear. But supposing you've plumped for a robust and unique, however memorable, master password which you haven't used somewhere else is really a near perfect approach to shield the remainder of one's passwords out of improper access.

Password supervisors do not only keep your passwords they Help you create and maintain strong, unique passwords whenever you register up to brand new sites. Meaning should you move to a site or program, you could pull your password up manager, copy your password, then glue it in the mailbox, and then you are in. Many times, password managers arrive with browser extensions which automatically complete your password to you.

And because most of those password supervisors outside there have Encoded sync across apparatus, you'll be able to simply take your passwords anywhere together on your own mobile phone.

Exactly why do you will need to make use of one?
Password supervisors take out the hassle of producing and Assessing strong passwords. It's that easy. However there are 3 good reasons why you should care.

Telephones are stolen all of the time. Internet sites and providers are At danger of breaches just as far as possible to phishing attacks which try to fool you in rotation within your own password. Even though organizations are intended to scramble your password if you input known as hashing -- perhaps not all of utilize modern or strong calculations, which makes it effortless for hackers to undo which hashing and then read your password in plaintext. Some businesses do not bother to hash in any way! This places your account in danger of fraud or your own computer data in danger to be properly used contrary to you for identity-theft.

However, the more and more complicated your password is a mixture of Uppercase and lower case characters, symbols, numbers and punctuation -- that the longer it can take for hackers to unscramble your password.

The other difficulty is that the absolute variety of passwords we've To recall. Banks, societal networking reports, our utilities and email -- it's simple to just use 1 password throughout the board. However, this produces"credential stuffing" easier. That is when hackers choose your password out of a broken website and attempt to sign into to your accounts on other websites. Utilizing a password manager which makes it much simpler to build and save stronger passwords which can be unique to every website, preventing credential stuffing strikes.

And, for the days you are at a busy or crowded area -- such as A coffeeshop or a plane -- consider who's just about you. Typing in passwords is observed, replicated and after used by local eavesdroppers. Utilizing a password manager in most instances eliminates the requirement to type some passwords whatsoever.

Which password manager if you utilize?

The easy answer is it's your decision. All password Managers perform mainly the exact duties -- but unique programs could have relevant or more features for you compared to others.

Anybody operating I-OS 1-1 or afterwards -- that can be iPhone and I-pad users will possess a password manager automagically so there isn't any explanation. You are able to sync your passwords around apparatus using I-Cloud key-chain.

For anybody else most password supervisors are liberated, together with all the Option to update to acquire superior features.

If You'd like your passwords to sync throughout apparatus for Example, LastPass is also a fantastic alternative. 1Password is trusted and incorporates with Troy Hunt's Pwned Passwords database, which means you may tell if (and prevent) A password that's been previously discharged or vulnerable at a data breach.

Many password supervisors are Cross Platform, such as Dashlane, Which also operate on mobile phones, letting you choose your passwords where you move.

And, a few are available source, such as KeePass, permitting anybody to Read the origin code. KeePass does not utilize the cloud therefore it leaves your computer if you don't proceed it. That is far better for its paranoid, but in addition for all those that may possibly face a larger array of dangers -- such as for example individuals who are employed in government.

Everything you might Discover helpful is that Rating of five password managers, that provides a breakdown through features.

Like most applications, vulnerabilities and flaws in almost any Password supervisor could create put your data in danger. But provided that you maintain your password boss up so far -- many browser extensions have been automatically upgraded -- that your hazard is somewhat reduced.

Password management for System owners

Password Strategies which may assist your organization stay secure.

Accounts coverage: upgrading your strategy

Password Policy: upgrading your approach comprises information for system owners accountable for discovering password policy. It might be of use too for anybody maintaining or developing these services utilized by businesses.

The NC SC Is employed to lessen businesses' reliance in their users being forced to remember massive variety of complex passwords. This guidance urges a larger dependence on technical defences along with organizational procedures, together with passwords forming only one-part of one's wider access control and identity management strategy.

Longer Namely this guidance may enable you :

- know the advantages and limits of passwords
- test and (if needed) question existing corporate password policies, and also help upgrade to your modern process
- know the decisions to be made after ascertaining password policy
- find out the way technical measures can cut back the password burden for your own users
- execute password policies that encourage the means that people naturally work
- enable users to produce and manage passwords which are more difficult to figure
- Note: Just as Something proprietor, you will well not Be accountable to your authentication processes within third-party services that your organization uses. In such scenarios, this guidance will be able to allow one to have an understanding of the advantages and pitfalls after picking these services, and also inform your range of 1 which best matches your company and security requirements.

Intro: the Issues with passwords

Bill Gates called that the passing of this password approximately 15 decades ago. Most supposed that alternative authentication techniques are adopted to restrain usage of IT infrastructure, data, and solutions. In reality, password usage has improved, and so they remain the default method of authentication to get a massive selection of services, either in home and work.

This Growth in password usage is chiefly due to this surge of internet services, Including those supplied by government and also the wider public industry, and also the Immense increase in usage of computers, smartphones and Tablets. Passwords are usually Regarded as an easily-implemented, cheap Security step since they don't need special hardware, together with obvious Attractions for supervisors within enterprise strategies.

But, This proliferation of password usage, and increasingly intricate password requirements, puts an unrealistic requirement for consumers. Inevitably, end users may invent their own working mechanisms to manage with 'password.' Attackers exploit these famous coping plans, leaving your organization and staff susceptible.

How are passwords located?

Attackers Make use of various methods to find passwords, harnessing a variety of societal and technical vulnerabilities. These comprise:

- tricking a person into revealing their password through social technologies (such as malware and coercion)

- Employing the passwords leaked out of information breaches to assault other programs by which users have utilized exactly the same password

- password spraying (having a Few commonly-used passwords within a attempt to get into a High Number of accounts)

- Brute-force strikes (the automatic imagining of substantial numbers of passwords before the right one is located)

- convicted of a password file, in which the hash could be broken to Recoup the initial passwords

- 'shoulder surfing' (celebrating Somebody typing into their password)

- discovering passwords That Have Been saved insecurely, for example sticky notes stored alongside some device, or files stored on apparatus

- guide password imagining (possibly using private information 'Automobiles' for example title, date of arrival, or even puppy titles)

- intercepting a password (or password) because It's transmitted over a system

- installing a keylogger to intercept passwords when they are input right into a device

All these Methods are commonly available and recorded on the World-wide web, and several utilize automated tools requiring only moderate technical competencies.

Passwords can just do this much

Passwords Have a restricted capability to secure your systems and data. When implemented properly, passwords have been not limited in helping prevent unauthorized access. When an attacker finds or guesses the password, then they have the ability to impersonate an individual. Less of course, every brand new password has a related burden on that the man with it.

Having Said that, there is lots you can do in order to ensure that your password policy is equally as effective as you can and incorporated in one's wider organizational way of authentication. The six hints explained in this advice Can Help You to:

- review the way your organization uses passwords
- receive the specialized controllers directly
- produce better consumer attention

Trick 1: Reduce your own business's dependence on Accounts

You will find Situation by which a password continues to be a suitable solution, such as usage of a guest wi-fi system. But, passwords are over used and implemented in lots of areas where they're perhaps not appropriate. A fantastic means to minimize password weight would be to just execute passwords once they're really appropriate and needed.

Technical Solutions (such as only sign-on) may also lower the load on staff. While these can incur any extra installation and managing expenses, they have been user friendly and enhance the entire system security, therefore can offer decent affordable in the long duration. Many devices already have biometric login options that can possibly be configured to make use of alternatively.

Utilize multi-factor authentication (MFA) for significant accounts

Certainly one of The best methods for providing additional security into some password-protected accounts is to utilize MFA. Accounts which were installed to make use of MFA require another variable, that will be something which you personally (and just you personally) may get. This might possibly be a code which is delivered for you by text, or that is created by means of an program, therefore even though an individual finds a password, then they won't find a way to get into the accounts without even compromising the different element. MFA is better used where there could be additional risk (for instance, logging into a free account on a fresh apparatus (internet-facing systems or to get priority reports). For more comprehensive information, consult with this nc-sc's assistance with Multi-factor authentication for internet services.

Use only sign-on systems

Single Sign-on (SSO) allows staff to make use of only 1 pair of certificate to automatically acquire entry to multiple software and solutions. Thus a user may login their work machine and also get access to what that they desire, without needing to input some other pair of credentials.

SSO can Simply take the shape of a online portal which authenticates an individual across almost all of their cloud services. This hugely reduces the pressure to get an individual to make and remember excellent passwords. But if an attacker compromises an individual's password or account, that attacker might have comfortable access to more content than that they have in a conventional system. Because of this, we urge that SSO be used to take MFA.

In Conclusion

- Simply utilize passwords where they're expected and proper
- Consider alternatives to passwords like SSO, hardware components and biometric solutions.
- Utilize MFA where potential for all essential accounts and online facing systems.

Trick 2: Employ technical answers

Your System's safety must consistently count upon effective technical defences as opposed to according to unachievableuser behavior. This section summarizes the technical solutions that your organization should implement directly (or try and see signs of if acquiring 3rd party services).

Use throttling or accounts lockout

Password Systems may be configured so that there's really a progressively increasing time delay between successive login attempts - a procedure referred to as 'throttling.' This limits the amount of suspects that an attacker may attempt while giving users a few chances to consider that their password. An option is accounts lockout, where an individual just includes a predetermined amount of efforts to manually input their password until their account is secured.

Throttling is advised, because accounts lockout can render valid users struggling to get into their account, and requires use of a account retrieval approach.

Account lockout could give an attacker having an simple solution to establish a denial of service attack, specially for large systems that are online.

When using accounts lockout, then we advise that you allow between 5 and 10 login attempts before the account is rooted, in order to prevent accidental lockout.

Security tracking

You will find Additional procedures for discovering and avoiding the abuse of account which could be viewed as along side accounts receivable (or lockout). By Way of Example, you can use collateral tracking to detect and alert you to that which might be indications of malicious or strange behavior, such like:

- Login efforts that neglect the next measure of MFA
- brute-forcing of accounts passwords, such as password spraying
- Login efforts out of sudden geographic places

Password Blacklisting

If users Are picking their passwords, a more very helpful defence is always to hire a password firewall which prevents the many typical (and consequently readily imagined) passwords used. In the event that you can not detach passwords at this point once they're manufactured, you may have the ability to retroactively hunt your password for those hashes of passwords that are blacklisted. If high quantities of shared passwords have been present, this really is a indication you should give users further aid managing and choosing their own passwords. Watch recommendations 45 and 6 for additional info.

A blacklist can be produced from the published lists of shared passwords or might be tailored to your own organization.

In Conclusion

- Utilize accounts lockout or throttling to shield against brute force attacks.
- When using lockout, allow users between 5 and 10 login attempts before locking out accounts.
- Contemplate using security tracking to shield against brute force attacks.
- Password blacklisting averts ordinary, guessable passwords used.

Trick 3: Protect passwords

Passwords Have to be guarded inside the human body, even when info on the secure platform is comparatively insignificant. Reuse of passwords implies an individual can use these records to make an effort to get more essential reports, where further damage might be accomplished.

This Section gives guidance for platform engineers and developers, and also certainly will help security professionals to choose those third-party systems and products which provide safer procedures of password processing and storage.

Protect passwords In-transit

Passwords Could be intercepted when in transit. To safeguard them you should make sure that most corporate web programs requiring authentication utilize HTTPS. A frequent sort of attack involves concealing a security amount to obtain use of some other server or device. 'dominate the hash' can be a typical illustration of the in which a stolen hash can be employed to authenticate the attacker. To learn more, choose into this nc-sc assistance with preventing lateral movement.

Take Care of the accessibility management program

The accessibility Management system should be shielded to stop attackers deploying it to obtain access to a own system (such as by altering password coverages, or decreasing tokens), if that is your organization or even a cloud or other internet support. As you can not alter the defences of these third-party approaches, you should take action to guard the access management approaches that you manage, and also you should discover how alternative party providers do the very same. For some more info, please consult with this nc-sc assistance with access and identity management.

Protect passwords in remainder

Ensure that you The systems that you set up don't save passwords as plain text, even when information on the secure system is relatively insignificant. Gently search systems such as password information that's stored in plaintext.

All Passwords must be kept in a hashed format, so with numerous iterations of this hash functionality. Hashing is really a one-time cryptographic function which transforms a plaintext password to some 'hash,' an unreadable series of characters made to be hopeless to convert. But, attackers may still utilize brute-force strikes and rainbow tables (precomputed tables such as Placing cryptographic hash functions) to recover passwords out of stolen hashes. Because of this, software should put in a 'salt' to a password before hashing. The hash function needs to follow people norms (for instance, PBKDF2), such as SHA 256.

An Whoever who has got a password file won't know the real passwords. However, in case the passwords are hashed badly, or so the attacker has enough computing power, it could be easy in order for them to regain a few of the passwords. Because of this it's necessary to get access into this consumer database. In addition to being a target for attackers seeking to undermine your own body, these certainly are a target inside their own right, even when info is old.

Prioritize procuring significant or Susceptible accounts

While all Passwords must be shielded, reports which have tremendously privileged use of systems, data and services (or reports that are reachable such as cloud remote or services access) are specifically popular with people. MFA are the keyway of protecting those balances. Imposing additional password complexity requirements on such account increases the load on those users, but might well not offer any further security.

Highly Privileged accounts must perhaps not be utilized for elevated risk or daily user pursuits, like getting outside email or surfing the World-wide web. For all these and other ordinary business use tasks, administrators also needs to provide standard user account (with various passwords).

Administrator Accounts for infrastructure apparatus can have pre-assembled passwords which is readily discovered. Because of this, all of default vendor-supplied passwords which have any system, applications or apparatus needs to be changed before installation. Trainers can assist hereby recording all of default passwords and explaining the way to alter them.

In Conclusion

- Make sure that most corporate web programs requiring authentication utilize HTTPS.
- Shield any access control systems that you can manage.
- Pick products and services which protect passwords with numerous iterations of a sterile cryptographic hash functionality.

- Protect access to consumer databases.
- Prioritize jobless and susceptible accounts such as receivers, cloud reports and distant customers.
- Change all default passwords.

Trick 4: Help customers deal with password

Users Have been told to consider passwords and to not share themre-use them or write down them. The issue with it is that the common user has heaps of passwords to consider -- not yours. To deal with this specific overload, users resort to workarounds, like reusing passwords, insecure storage or foreseeable passwords. This section explains how your organization may offer sanctioned mechanisms to aid users manage passwords there is less incentive to embrace speculative work arounds.

Utilize password management applications or other protected Storage

Now you Should offer suitable facilities to save passwords. The nc-sc urge the usage of password managers for storage where appropriate. In addition to providing stable storage, password managers may help users from generating and auto-filling passwords once demanded. We urge that most internet providers enable the usage of password managers, and also that users should really be permitted to glue passwords to web forms. But like every piece of security applications, password managers aren't impregnable and so are still an attractive target for attackers. To Find out More, consult with this NC SC Password Manager Buyers Guide.

In case Your Password supervisor isn't suitable you should offer physical storage for listed passwords such as for example a secure cabinet. You can also require stable storage to get MFA tokens. This ought to be different from the password.

Do not apply routine password

Routine Password altering accidents instead of improves security. Many systems will induce users to modify their password at regular intervals, on average every 30, 60 or even 90 days. This avoids burdens on an individual as well as also there are costs related to regaining reports.

Forcing Password includes no genuine benefits as:

- an individual is very likely to decide on new passwords which are only slight variations of their older
- stolen passwords are usually tapped instantly

- resetting the password provides you no information regarding if or not a compromise has happened
- a attacker using this accounts will receive the petition to reset the password
- if endangered via insecure storage, then the attacker should have the ability to come across the new password at precisely the exact same place

As an Alternative Of pushing expiry, you ought to offset the illegal usage of passwords that are compromised :

- assuring a successful movers/leavers process is in place
- mechanically locking out inactive accounts
- tracking logins for questionable behavior (for instance, odd login times, logins using new apparatus)
- inviting users to record if something's questionable

You are able to Additionally mitigate the probability of endangered accounts using MFA, that may produce a compromised password not as useful for an attacker. Some MFA techniques (for instance, SMS or email notifications) may additionally warn the user they've now been compromised, since they are going to be given a code whenever they failed to ask it. If you're employing this sort of MFA, you should encourage end users to record that behavior throughout your training.

Note: Users must change their passwords whenever you understand (or guess) it was endangered.

Managing shared accessibility

Sharing Work reports, if not intermittent usage by anybody apart from the account holder, even introduces lots of risks. In addition to the chance of users obtaining access to unauthorized tools, sharing balances interrupts the advantage of authenticating a particular user. Specifically, the capacity to audit and track a particular user's activities has been lost, an crucial forensic requirement for a number of accounts.

In case Passwords have been shared, decide to try and discover alternative solutions that encourage the company requirement for sharing. By way of instance, a lot of accounts are going to have means to assign privileges to some other accounts (for instance, usage of a record or in box). Delegation needs to be utilized rather than sharing reports where possible.

In case Alternatives aren't possible, and there still is a solid business requirement for shared usage of a account or apparatus, then usage of this password needs to be tracked and reviewed to handle the danger:

- the password should only be shared over the lowest possible set of trusted and known clients
- the password should not be confronted with users who don't need consent to get this
- if some body is no more granted access the password ought to be changed

Some Password supervisors enable users to talk about passwords at a safer way (as an instance, they could audit usage of the password and also mechanically sync password shifts). When you own a business should share with you a password then look at making use of a password manager to get this done.

In Conclusion

- Users possess an entire bundle of passwords to handle, and not yours.
- Let users to safely store their own passwords.
- Just ask end users to modify their passwords indication or feeling of compromise.

- Utilize delegation tools rather than password sharing.

Trick 5: enable users to create Improved passwords

Passwords Could be made by the consumer, or else they might be supplied for them with an agency. Both techniques have advantages and pitfalls that you'll have to think about when deciding upon a way. In any event, if you're depending just on the effectiveness of your own passwords (either user or machine generated) your system will stay vulnerable to a lot of strikes. You ought to make use of the extra defences discussed previously to present nearly all one's protection against a variety of strikes.

Implementing machine-generated passwords

Machine-generated Passwords remove those passwords which could be simple for a person to assume. They require minimal effort from an individual to make, and may produce passwords which can be arbitrary and unique. But most machine-generated passwords have become tough for visitors to keep in mind. Because of this, the nc-sc urge they ought to be employed using a password manager. Most password managers include things like a random password generator, and staff ought to be invited to make use of this where possible.

Since Machine-generated passwords are tough for folks to consider, with them without a password manager gains:

- that the expenditures involved with providing account retrieval for abandoned passwords
- the probability of users embracing insecure work-arounds

Ideally, When having a machine-generated password without a password manager, the machine needs to provide users a selection of passwords (therefore that they are able to choose the one that they find that the many remarkable), or produce CVC-CVC-CVC (consonant-vowel-consonant) style passwords which are easier to keep in mind. But, you ought to assume that the individual may learn the arrangement that you employ, and can correct their attack consequently.

Dealing Together with user-generated passwords

User-generated Accounts are fast and simple to execute, and so are definitely the most frequent method of writing passwords. But they take dangers that machine-generated passwords don't

- users can reuse passwords they use on additional programs
- users can utilize easily guessed passwords (such as a pet's name)
- users can embrace predictable password creation approaches (like replacing the letter 'o' using a zero)

This Means that methods using user-generated passwords will normally contain a high quantity of passwords which will beginto fall into an automatic guessing attack. Password blacklisting might help prevent the most frequent passwords used.

Password Grid meters intention to help users measure the strength in their self generated passwords. They can steer you far from the accounts that are weakest, but frequently don't account fully for the aspects which could cause guessable passwords (for instance, using personal info, or even replicating characters or shared character strings).

You ought to know about these limits if using password-strength meters.

Don't utilize sophistication requirements

Using Sophistication requirements (which is(where employees can simply use passwords which are appropriately complex) is really a bad defence against guessing attacks. It puts an excess burden for users, a lot of whom can utilize predictable patterns (for instance, replacing the letter 'o' with a zero) to fulfill up with the mandatory 'sophistication' criteria. Attackers are familiarized with those plans and make use of this awareness to reevaluate their strikes. In addition, sophistication requirements offer no defence against common attack types like social technologies or insufficient storage of passwords.

For your Above reasons, the nc-sc do perhaps not recommend using sophistication requirements when employing consumer passwords that are generated. Using controls to shield against automated guessing attacks is a lot more powerful than counting on users to build (and remember) passwords that are complex. But, you need to define a minimum password length, to stop very short passwords from being properly used. Avoid any maximum amount requirements a user may decide to try to transcend, since they are going to make it tougher for users to opt for the right password that suits the length criteria. Password span should just be restricted by the capacities of your own body. Be conscious that employing too long passwords will present different burdens (for instance, time required to input passwords, and also the higher odds of mistyping notably on touch screen apparatus). Assessing the three arbitrary words' technique may enable users to utilize appropriately complex passphrases they are able to remember.

In Conclusion

- Be conscious of the advantages and disadvantages of password creation procedures.
- When password managers are all used, encourage using their built-in password generator.
- Complexity conditions offer no defence against common attacks and must not be utilized.
- Avoid users setting passwords which are too short.
- Do not inflict artificial capping on password length.

Your Existing training could contain giving users an easy lists of dos and also performn 'ts.' This sounds sensible, however it might be counter productive since the information might contradict what they have heard everywhere, and may lead to confusion. As an alternative, your practice should revolve around things which can actually improve security. These comprise:

- emphasizing the dangers involved with using exactly the Exact passwords over house and operate balances
- assisting users to produce passwords which can not be readily imagined; instruction may emphasize the significance of preventing personal information (like titles, dates, along with sports groups)
- Employing the 3 arbitrary words strategy to assist users produce significantly less predictable passwords
- training team how to utilize password supervisors (if you are using them), such as Features like the password generator

Helps users to Control the password load

You will find Numerous ways in which you may assist your team to control their passwords:

- permit methods which can be low hazard (as an instance, secure storage or staying logged in)
- provide tailored guidance that is possible for users to get and put into actions

- ensure users know that of the balances are of high priority
- provide users with the training or tools that they will need to guard them priority accounts (as an instance MFA, ensuring staff have logged out)

Managing consumer statements

Giving users Un-necessary system rights or information accessibility Rights implies that in case the account is compromised or endangered the impact is likely to be more acute than it must be.

Overview

When users are Given unnecessary system rights or Data access rights, and then the effect of abuse or compromise of this users accounts will probably undoubtedly be more acute than it necessary. All of us should be offered with a fair (but minimal) degree of system rights and privileges required for their own role. The awarding of exceptionally elevated system privileges needs to be carefully controlled and handled. This principle may be called 'least privilege.'

What's the chance?

Organizations need to know the degree of accessibility Employees will need to advise, resources and services to be able to do their own occupation differently it's not going to be possible to take care of rights suitably. Struggling to effortlessly manage user statements could lead to the next risks being realised:

- Misuse of Evidence: Users may either intentionally or intentionally abuse the rights assigned to these. This might cause unauthorized usage of information regarding the consumer or even a 3rd party or into unauthorized system changes using immediate security or operational effects.

- Improved offender capability: Attackers can use compromised or malicious user account to undertake strikes and, even when possible, they can go back to recreate the endangered account or potentially sell usage of others. The machine rights supplied to the very first user of these endangered accounts will probably be open to the consumer to make use of that will be the reason why they specially try to acquire use of exceptionally authorized or administrative reports.

- Negating established security controllers: Where aliens have privileged system access they can make changes to security controllers make it possible for future or further attack or may try to cover their tracks by making audit or changing logs.
- Just how does the risk be handled?
- Organizations need to ascertain what rights and rights Users will need to efficiently execute their responsibilities and execute a policy of 'least privilege.'

Establish powerful account management Procedures: Handle user accounts out of production, through-life and revocation if a part of staff leaves or shifts role. Bookmarking accounts, perhaps given for temporary staff or for analyzing, needs to be suspended or removed if no more demanded.

Establish policies and criteria for consumer Authentication and access control: A business password policy ought to be established that hunts a powerful balance between usability and security as put down within our password guidance. For a few accounts that an extra authentication variable (for instance, a token) maybe appropriate.

Limit user statements: Users must be provided together with the Fair minimum rights Along with permissions to approaches, information and services they will need to satisfy their organization role.

Limit the amount and use of accounts: only restrain the awarding of exceptionally commended system Rights, estimating the continuing dependence regularly. Highly privileged administrative reports must not be utilized for elevated risk or day-to-day user pursuits, such as web surfing and email. Administrators should make use of normal makes up about standard small business usage.

Monitor: Monitor User action, specially usage of sensitive information and also using privileged accounts activities. Respond where tasks are out normal, expected boundaries (for instance, usage of considerable numbers of sensitive information out standard working hours).

Limit accessibility into this partitioning method and also the machine Activity logs: Action logs from system apparatus should be routed to a passionate bookkeeping and audit system that's separated by the center system. Usage of the audit system and also the logs needs to be rigorously controlled to keep the integrity of their content and most of privileged consumer access listed.

Educate consumers and keep their consciousness: All consumers should Know about the policy concerning suitable Account use and their individual duty to abide by corporate security policies.

Ranning User Accounts & Passwords

All these are Front line security problems with an immediate effect on how that you handle your own personal data, such as user passwords and accounts.

DO's And DON'Ts for handling passwords & accounts

DO'S

- Utilize a password using a mixture of eight mixed-case alphabetic characters, numerals and special characters.
- Use a password that's hard to guess but easy for you to consider, and therefore you don't need to write down it.
- Utilize a password which you can type quickly, without being forced to examine the computer keyboard, hence preventing passersby seeing exactly what you're currently typing.

- Change your password often, at least one-time every ninety days.
- Change the default initial password the first time you login.
- Create a solid authentication mechanism, such as for instance two-factor authentication, for user account which handle sensitive data.
- Utilize different passwords for various accounts, specifically individuals for handling sensitive and private data.
- Change your password immediately in the event that you think it is often compromised. Once done, inform the system/security administrator to followup actions.
- Log off when finished using terminals or PCs in public places, like a cafe or library.

DON'TS

- Do not use your name for a login name in any sort (Asis, reversed, capitalized, doubled, and so forth).
- Do not utilize the title of your partner or kid in almost any kind.
- Do not use other information which may be readily obtained about you personally. Including ID card numbers, license numbers, telephone numbers and

birth dates, and the name of this road you survive, etc.

- Do not use a password which comprises all digits, or all of the exact letters.
- Do not use a phrase Which Can Be found in a British or Language dictionary.
- Do not use a phrase in reverse Which Can Be found in a British or foreign language dictionary.
- Do not utilize a renowned abbreviation e.g. HKSAR, HKMA, MTR.
- Do not reuse passwords that are recently used.
- Do not utilize the exact same password for all; have a password to get non critical pursuits and also another for sensitive or significant pursuits.
- Do not take note of your password, specially anywhere near your pc or document it into a box with the word 'password' written onto it.
- Do not let or give your passwords out into others, even for an Excellent reason.
- Do not show your password to the screen.
- Do not ship your password especially via email.
- Prevent working with the "remember that the password" feature connected to a few internet sites, also disable this feature on your browser program.

- Do not save your password on any network unless it's protected from unauthorized access (e.g. encrypted using a licensed encryption system).

The Listed below are several security methods that could help system/security administrators in tackling Document selection criteria.

Do's And Cann'ts for system/security staff

DO'S

- Choose good passwords initial passwords for your accounts.
- Use various passwords as passwords for various accounts.
- Ask users alter the password instantly upon getting the password.
- Change all of system default passwords, for example service balances after installing a brand new platform.
- Request users to modify their passwords occasionally, at the very least one-time every 90 days.

- Simply suspend an individual accounts following a pre-determined variety of invalid login attempts.

- Restrict a frozen accounts to simply permit reactivation by guide actions regulated by the system/security administrator.

- Prevent users by using passwords briefer compared to the usual pre-defined span, or reusing used or old passwords.

DON'TS

- Do not send unencrypted passwords especially via email.

- Do not reset or disclose passwords behalf of users that are unknown.

- Do not allow community access into a password management, such as UNIX password records.

CHAPTER FIVE
PENETRATION TESTING

Penetration Testing, also referred to as pencil testing or ethical hacking, maybe the custom of analyzing A computer program, network or web application to seek out security vulnerabilities That the attacker can tap. Penetration testing may be automatic with Software programs or performed by hand.

The User gained access into This Fortune 500 financial Services firm via an older, half-forgotten Siemens-Rolm PBX (Private Branch Exchange) telecom management program. System administrators at the company'd changed the administrative accounts password, however they had forgotten or never knew regarding the factory-installed field tech accounts on this system. This password has been set to the default value, only because it had been around countless of additional similar machines round the whole world.

The PBX was attached to the company's Voice Mail program, however To not the considerably more sensitive critical fiscal control and human capital systems. Those systems have been safe, secured behind a Check Point firewall and only accessible via secure two-factor authentication systems, closely tracked, and also with the most recent security patches installed.

The hacker was patient and smart, though. He discovered the Voice mailbox to your own IT help desk, cloned into some that he can assess. Waited. Listened.

An individual called in 1 afternoon, having difficulty getting in on his VPN (Virtual Private Network) account. The hacker functioned fast. He even deleted the message from the valid IT help desk voicemail," known as an individual himself back and readily acquired the password along with onetime authentication token him off. The user subsequently helped an individual mend his trouble, to allay any suspicions that the guy could happen to be.

By there, the hacker's logged on the User accounts himself was crying through the interior system, owning host after host, the keys to the realm in his palms on.

Weeks afterwards, the IT Help Desk supervisor obtained a high-value letter From that particular user. The consumer commended that the technician which had helped him along with his VPN problem a few of weeks ago, describing him polite, smart and quick.

The only difficulty was, that the Help Desk manager had never discovered Of the technology. Do not have anybody working there by this name. Providentially, that the CIO (Chief Information Officer) knew who it was. Even the"hacker" has been a penetration tester hired by the business to locate and exploit some vulnerabilities in their own systems... until the hackers can perform so.

Penetration testing may be the most visible element of What network safety auditors perform, however the stark reality is that cyber-security professionals participate near-constant cycles of testing and assessment. This creates learning how to assess hazard and shield against it a seriously significant part a cyber-security level app.

Weighing the Risks at Modern Information Systems

Cyber-security evaluations fall into two broad classes:

- Risk evaluations
- Vulnerability assessments

Risk is a phrase with a very special meaning within the Realm of data security and it is usually misunderstood beyond the area. Risk is the possibility of a loss multiplied by the chances of this loss occurring. However perceptions of hazard are often colored by fear, anxiety, and doubt, inducing chances and results to be or undervalued centered on factors such as networking policy or a individual's emotion.

Cloud-based Techniques, as an Example, are always Regarded to be less stable than on-premises procedures, even though the majority of the statistics available prove differently. Still, the majority of men and women have a tendency to feel that data behind a door that is locked is safe provided that they hold the important thing, even when that is maybe not effortlessly the instance.

Because these trivial variables can make it hard For cyber-security experts to accurately assess hazard, the National Institutes of Science and Technology (NIST) allow us a cyber-security frame which enables you to assess threats to critical infrastructure as well as provide pragmatic procedural and policy mitigations. Cyber-security analysts utilize such frameworks to operate with security engineers and key operators to appraise prospective goals within the organization information system and set the chance of compromise.
Besides this comparatively simple variables of Costs from lost earnings and episode response out of potential

breaches, security analysts may additionally need to await more esoteric elements like lack in consumer confidence and potential customer suits. In the aftermath of some 2014 theft of customer details, Target Corporation settled nearly $120 million in legal settlements along with internal retrieval expenses. In the event the dangers of compromise was satisfactorily assessed before that thieving, the corporation might have spent more than $100 million in security measures but come out far ahead at the long ran.

A threat evaluation, then, points into the systems where Vulnerabilities may possibly be less devastating should used. This permits the cyber-security auditor to focus resources where they'll be useful in discovering vulnerabilities.

Isolating the Flaws Through Penetration Testing
Vulnerability evaluations, or Tests, assess what Specific risks exist at the present system arrangement.

Standard audits are a Great clinic for any Info Security group however in some businesses, they are falsified and/or ran by regulatory agencies. HIPAA, the medical insurance Portability and Accountability Act, for example, claims strict scrutiny standards for healthcare providers and carriers. And the Security and Exchange Commission's audits of fiscal aid providers today comprises a cyber-security Examination Initiative that resembles information security methods.

The sharpest tool in the vulnerability evaluation Tool Box Is your penetration evaluation, or"pencil evaluation " Penetration testing involves cyber-security teams (called "tiger teams") accepting the use of blackhat hackers and also attempting to access resources or data through activities that could otherwise be illegal. Penetration testers have employed:

- Social engineering
- Automated scanners
- Password breaking tools
- Other frequent Black Hat manipulation tools

Penetration testing parameters are all set by the thing Asking the evaluations, therefore loopholes that could bring about the disturbance of services or even destruction of information could be illegal. Nevertheless, in any respect pen-testers utilize precisely the exact same devious bag of suggestions which valid cyber-criminals may possibly utilize. The purpose is to come across every one the vulnerabilities that attackers could exploit.

Automating Penetration Testing

While pencil analyzing could be spectacular, in training it's more a Random photo of vulnerability compared to the consistent, reproducible appraisal mechanism. But, certain pencil testing applications, like the Nessus scanner, that may automatically scan a system for known vulnerabilities, could be conducted regularly to capture any famous setup flaws and alarm security engineers.

Logs are just another important tool utilized in community safety auditing. The character of contemporary cyber-attacks is to render a few hints which could be reclined into the typical user. However, no activity needs to escape the eyes of a precisely configured charging apparatus. Even though modern intrusion detection systems might be programmed to block traffic, there's always the prospect of a brand new hazard with ribbons which have not been diagnosed yet.

Log analytics applications, for example Splunk, will help discover "imperceptible" strikes by searching for traffic that's only out from the ordinary. Once every ordinary and answerable activity is filtered outside, expert systems or cyber-security analysts may examine logs for signs of unlawful activity.

All of the processes utilized to ascertain danger and Vulnerability, it's really a cyber-security truism which you don't know exactly what to shield against if you don't know what it is that you're protecting... such as an older, half-forgotten PBX platform with an default tech account at the trank.

What's Penetration Testing?

It sounds Like every single day dawns with a brand new headline about the latest cyber-security attack. Hackers are still steal tens of thousands of records along with countless dollars in a alarming frequency. The real key to fighting their efforts would be to ran comprehensive insight evaluations through the entire season.

Penetration testing is designed to evaluate your Security before a person will. Penetration testing applications simulate real-life attack situations to detect and exploit security gaps which may result in discharged records, endangered credentials, intellectual property, personally identifiable information (PII), cardholder data, personal, protected health data, data ransom, or other detrimental small business outcomes. By exploiting security vulnerabilities, penetration testing makes it possible to determine the way you can best mitigate and secure your vital company data from prospective cyber-security strikes.

How Do You Harness Vulnerabilities?

Penetration Testing may be achieved in-house by your experts using pencil testing applications, or you may out source into an insight testing services provider. A penetration evaluation begins with the security practitioner enumerating the mark system to discover vulnerable accounts or systems. This means assessing each platform onto the system for open ports which have services ranning in it. It's rather rare that the whole system has every single service configured properly, correctly password-protected, and fully repaired. Once the penetration expert comes with a fantastic comprehension of the network and also the vulnerabilities which can be found, she or he use a penetration testing tool to exploit vulnerability as a way to acquire unwelcomed gain access.

Security Professionals usually don't just aim systems, nevertheless. Many times, a pencil tester aims users onto a system through malicious emails, pretext calling, or on site societal technology.

How Can You Exam the "User Risk" For Your IT Security Chain?

Your Users pose an extra hazard factor too. Attacking a system via human error or compromised credentials is not anything fresh. In the event the continuous cyber-security strikes and data breaches have taught us anything, it's the simplest method to get a hacker to go into a system and steal funds or data would be still through users.

Compromised Credentials are the best attack vector around reported data breaches year in, year out, a fad proven by the Verizon Data Breach Report. Section of a penetration evaluation's project is to fix the above security hazard due to user error. A pencil tester will attempt brute-force password imagining of accounts that are discovered to access applications and systems. While compromising 1 system may result in a violation, at a real-life situation an attacker may on average utilize lateral movement to finally land onto a crucial advantage.

Still another Common means to check the security of your system users is by way of a simulated malware assault. Phishing attacks utilize customized communicating techniques to convince the prospective to take action that is not in their very best interest. As an instance, a malware attack may convince an individual it's time for a"compulsory password-reset" also to click an embedded email connection. Whether simply clicking the malicious connection drops it or malware only provides the attacker the entranceway that they will need to slip certificate for prospective usage, then a phishing attack is just one of the simplest approaches to exploit users. If you're wanting to examine your users' consciousness about malware attacks, be certain the penetration testing tool that you utilize has these capacities.

What Exactly Does Penetration Testing Requires to some Company?

A Penetration evaluation is a vital element of network security. During those evaluations that a business can recognize:

- Security vulnerabilities before a hacker does
- Gaps in data security compliance
- The reply period of These data security staff, i.e. just how long it requires the staff to Understand That There's a violation and mitigate the effect

The Possible Real World impact of an information breach or Cyber-security assault

Actionable remediation advice

Throughout Performance testing, security professionals can effortlessly find and examine the security of multi-tier system architectures, custom software, services, along with other IT components. These penetration testing programs and tools assist you to gain fast insight into the fields of highest hazard therefore you might effortlessly organize security budgets and endeavors. Thoroughly analyzing the conclusion of a firm's IT infrastructure is crucial to carrying the steps required to safeguard vital data from cyber-security hackers, even while simultaneously improving the response time of an IT section in case of an attack.

Businesses do everything they can to safeguard their Critical cyber assets, however they do not always systematically examine their defenses. Penetration evaluations -- otherwise called pencil tests -- really are a kind of ethical hacking used to regularly measure the security of a system. Our crew of highly-skilled cyber-security pros uses a mixture of strategic and tactical ways to detect and exploit vulnerabilities on your IT systems.

Whether We're analyzing a program or system Environment, trip-wire's pencil testing won't merely identify vulnerabilities, although it is going to even demonstrate them during manipulation -- liberally determining if unauthorized access or other malicious activity could be potential.

A Penetration Tester (a.k.a. Pen Tester or Ethical Hacker) probes for and exploits security vulnerabilities in on-line software, systems and networks. In other words, you receive money to lawfully hack. Within this fascinating project, you have to employ a streak of insight tools -- a few pre-determined, something which you design -- to mimic real-time cyber strikes. Your final purpose is always to help a business improve its security.

Ethical Hacking is a variety of sexiness and dull pieces. Unlike hackers, you might just have days to undermine strategies. Moreover, you're going to be likely to record and explain your findings and methods. Penetration testing was called one of the most bothersome work inside the infosec field, however it is among the very creative. You should have tons of chances to apply your technical skills and you should always be considering your own feet.

Penetration Tester Job Responsibilities

Throughout The penetration evaluation, you may typically center on exploiting vulnerabilities (e.g. rendering it a wish to break a portion of a method). However, as Daniel Miessler Highlights from The Big Difference Between a Vulnerability Assessment and also a Penetration Evaluation, you do not need to really go All of the way to prove your purpose:

"A Penetration testing crew could find a way to just shoot images standing alongside the open safe to reveal they will have full usage of some database, etc., without taking the comprehensive collection of activities which a criminal may."

In General, You're inclined to be needed to:

- Perform proper penetration evaluations on web-based applications, networks and pcs
- Conduct physical security evaluations of servers, network and systems apparatus
- Layout and make fresh insight tools and evaluations
- Probe for vulnerabilities in web software, fat/thin client software and conventional software
- pin-point techniques that attackers might use to exploit flaws and logic flaws
- Employ interpersonal technologies to discover security holes (e.g. inferior user security techniques or password coverages)

- Contain business factors (e.g. lack in earnings because of downtime, and cost of participation, etc..) into security plans

- research, record and share security findings with direction and IT teams

- Inspection and specify requirements for information security solutions

- Function on developments to security solutions, like the continuous enhancement of present methodology material along with encouraging assets

- Supply feedback and confirmation within a firm fixes security problems

- Penetration testing, also known as pencil ethical or testing Hacking, maybe the custom of analyzing a computer system, system or web application to seek out security vulnerabilities an attacker may tap. Penetration testing may also be automated with applications or performed by hand. In any event, the method involves collecting information regarding the target ahead of the evaluation, pinpointing potential entrance points, wanting to split -- virtually or for real reporting and -- the findings back.

The Main Goal of penetration testing would be to spot Security flaws. Penetration testing may be employed to check a company's security policy, its adherence to compliance requirements, its employees' security knowledge and also the business's capability to spot and respond to security events.

Typically, the Information Regarding safety flaws that Are recognized or manipulated through pencil testing is aggregated and supplied to the company's IT and network platform managers, allowing them to make tactical decisions and enhance remediation efforts.

Penetration tests are also occasionally called White-hat Strikes because in a pencil test, the decent guys working hard to crack in.

Role of immersion testing

The Main Objective of a pencil evaluation will be to identify weak areas in A firm's security position, in addition to quantify the compliance of its security policy, examine the team's understanding of security problems and also determine if -- and how -- that the company could be at the mercy of security disasters.

A penetration test may additionally highlight flaws within an Company's safety policies. For example, though a security policy concentrates on preventing and discovering an attack within a business's systems, this policy might not include an activity to neutralize an individual hacker.

The Reports created by means of a penetration evaluation supply the feedback required for a company to reevaluate the investments it intends to create in its own security. These reports may also help application developers create more protected programs. If programmers comprehend how hackers jumped in the software they helped grow, the purpose is to inspire programmers to boost their instruction around security in order that they won't create exactly the exact same or equivalent errors later on.

Just how often you need to do penetration testing

Businesses Should perform pencil testing regularly -- once annually -- to make sure greater consistent network security and IT management. Along with ranning regulatory-mandated investigation and tests, penetration tests might also be conducted through a business:

- adds fresh system infrastructure or software;
- makes significant upgrades or alterations to its infrastructure or applications;
- specifies offices in new locations;
- implements security spots; or even

- modifies end user policies.

But, Because penetration testing isn't one-size-fits-all, as soon as a corporation should take part in pencil testing additionally depends on a lot of different elements, for example:

how big is the business. Businesses with a bigger presence on the web tend significantly more attack vectors and, for that reason, are more-attractive goals for hackers.

Penetration evaluations can be expensive, so an organization with an inferior funding may possibly not have the capability to ran them yearly. An company with bigger funding could just have the ability to ran a penetration test once every 2 years as an organization with a bigger budget could perform penetration testing annually.

Regulations and compliance. Businesses in some specific businesses are expected by law to execute certain security activities, including pencil analyzing.

A business whose infrastructure is at the cloud may perhaps not be permitted to try the cloud provider's infrastructure. Nevertheless, the provider could be ranning pencil tests.

Penetration Testing attempts needs to be tailored to the respective company in addition to a it works in and may consist of evaluation and follow-up tasks therefore your vulnerabilities contained in the most recent pencil evaluation are note recorded in following evaluations.

Penetration testing applications

Pen Testers frequently use automatic tools to find conventional application vulnerabilities. Pen testing applications examine data encryption methods and may identify hardcoded values, like user names and passwords, to support safety vulnerabilities from the computer system.

Penetration Testing tools ought to:

- be simple to deploy, use and configure;
- scan a method readily;
- categorize vulnerabilities dependent upon seriousness, i.e., the ones which will need to get repaired instantly;
- allow you to accomplishing the confirmation of vulnerabilities;
- re-verify past loopholes; along with
- generate detailed vulnerability logs and reports.

A lot of The very widely used penetration testing applications are all free or open-source software; that gives pencil testers the capability to alter or adapt the code to their needs. A number of the very frequently used open or free source pen-testing programs involve:

- The Metasploit Project can be a open-source project possessed by the security company Rapid7, that permits full-featured variants of their Metasploit applications. It hastens popular penetration testing applications which may be applied to servers, online-based networks and applications. Metasploit may be utilized to detect safety difficulties, to check vulnerability mitigations also to manage security procedures.
- Nmap, short for "system mapper," is really a port scanner which scans networks and systems for vulnerabilities connected to ports that are open. Nmap is led for the IP addresses or address which the network or system to be scanned can be found and tests all those systems for open interfaces; additionally, Nmap is utilized to track service or host Upgrades and map system attack environments.
- Wireshark can be actually a tool for social traffic and also for analyzing network programs. Wireshark empowers businesses to observe that the smaller

details about their system tasks occurring inside their own networks. This insight tool is really a system analyzer/network sniffer/network protocol analyzer that assesses vulnerabilities in network traffic in real-time. Wireshark is frequently utilized to inspect the information on traffic in various degrees.

- John the Ripper integrates different password crackers into a package, mechanically explains various kinds of password hashes and determines that a customizable cracker. Pen testers on average make use of the application to establish strikes to seek out password flaws in databases or systems.

Penetration Testers utilize a number of the very same tools that blackhat hackers utilize, partly because those tools are somewhat well-documented and widely offered, but also as it assists the pencil adjuster to understand the way those tools could be summoned contrary to their associations.

Penetration test plans

One Crucial facet of almost any penetration testing application is defining the exact extent where the pencil trainee must function. Usually, the scope defines exactly what approaches, locations, tools and techniques can be utilized at a penetration test. Limiting the reach of the penetration evaluation helps team associates and defenders on both systems across the company has controller.

By Way of Example, if penetration anglers Access some system Because a worker abandoned a password in plain sight, so which shows lousy security methods on the portion of the employee; it provides the pencil testing team no more insights into the security of this application form which has been endangered.

Here are several of the Primary pencil test approaches used by Security pros:

Targeted testing Is done by the company's IT team and also the penetration testing team working together. It's sometimes known as a"lights flipped out" approach because everybody else is able to observe the evaluation being performed out.

Topical testing aims A organization's externally observable servers or apparatus including domain servers, email servers, web servers or firewalls. The target is to learn if some other attacker can be in and how they could be in whenever they will have gained access.

Internal analyzing Mimics an interior attack behind the firewall with an official user using conventional access rights. This sort of evaluation is useful for estimating just how much damage a dissatisfied employee can cause.

Blind analyzing simulates The activities and procedures of a true attacker by severely limiting the data supplied to the individual or team performing the evaluation ahead. On average, the pencil adjuster might just receive the name of the business. Because this kind of evaluation may take a substantial period of time for reconnaissance, it might be costly.

Double-blind testing normally takes the blind evaluation also takes it a step farther. Inside This type of Pencil evaluation, merely a couple of different people within the company may bear in mind that a test has been ran. Double-blind tests might be helpful for analyzing a company's security tracking and incident identification in addition to its answer procedures.

Blackbox testing Is essentially exactly the like blind testing, nevertheless the tester receives no more advice before the evaluation occurs. Rather, the pencil testers must discover their own way into the computer system.

White-box testing supplies The penetration testers details about the prospective system till they start their job. This information may contain such details since IP addresses, system infrastructure schematics along with also the protocols used in addition to the origin code.

Employing distinct pencil testing approaches helps pencil testing Teams concentrate on the systems that are desired and gain insight to the forms of strikes which are most threatening.

CHAPTER SIX
CYBER RISK ASSESSMENT AND MANAGEMENT

Risk Direction is a continuous process which involves identifying, assessing and reacting to danger. When tackling hazard, ostensibly there are four strategies to accomplish this, for example mitigating the hazard, moving it, steering clear of the probability or taking it.

Cyber Hazard isn't any risk related to financial loss, disruption to operations or injury to an organization's standing in the negative event affecting the organization's advice and/or advice systems.

Cases Include cyber-crime, data breaches and network outages to list a couple. Effective cyber hazard control is significantly more than firewalls, log tracking or deploying anti-virus applications. It needs a holistic perspective of people, products and processes to architect a more stable, resilient and efficient organization. As technology gets profoundly ingrained in what we do so when businesses are more reliant upon it, the cyber-security threat landscape always affects making managing cyber hazard a lot complex. Assessing and executing the proper mixture of people, product and process, balancing risk and benefit and Assessing the return on investment in security measures can be a struggle for some businesses. We help businesses to control their own risk, we do so by leveraging our years of knowledge of deploying and managing proven, practical, pragmatic, more successful and cost-effective IT Security programs to a lot of organizations over many diverse businesses.

Risk Has favorable aspects when handled properly competitive advantage, industry growth and sales expansion to list a couple.

Can be Your organization ready for a cyber-security violation?

Your Information has worth, personally identifiable data, intellectual property, trade secrets and advice regarding calls, mergers and prices are typical tempting targets for attackers. An info breach could have lots of impacts, as an instance, commercial declines, people relations issues, disruption to business operations and also the chance of extortion. A cyberattack might even introduce your organization to regulatory actions, neglect claims, the inability to satisfy contractual duties and also a damaging lack of confidence among clients and providers as your standing is affected.

Cyber Hazard is actually a constantly increasing hazard for the organization's capability to reach its own objectives and deliver to its business objectives. One powerful attack might have a catastrophic impact on your own organization's financial status and standing.

What's hazard?

Risk is The probability of reputational or monetary loss and will be step from, low, moderate, to high quality. The 3 facets which feed to some hazard vulnerability assessment are:

what's the hazard?
How exposed is your machine?
What's the reputational or monetary harm if violated or left inaccessible?
This Gives us a of cyber hazard like: Cyber hazard = Threat x Vulnerability x Info Worth

Imagine You should gauge the hazard connected with a cyber-attack undermining a specific os. This operating system comes with a famous anti-virus in version 1.7 of its applications that's readily exploitable via physical stores and means information about top value onto it. If a workplace does not have any actual security, your risk could be quite high.

But, When you've got good IT staff that is able to identify vulnerabilities and so they upgrade the os to version 1.8, your exposure is reduced, although the information value continues to be high since the backend has been patched in version 1.8.

Some Matters to bear in mind is that there are hardly any matters without a risk to some company approach or information strategy, and hazard indicates doubt. When something is certainto take place, it isn't just a risk. It's a portion of overall company operations.

What's a cyber hazard appraisal?

Cyber Hazard evaluations are characterized by NIST as risks evaluations are utilized to identify, quote, and reevaluate risk to organizational operations, organizational resources, individuals, other associations, and also the country, leading from the surgery and usage of information methods.

The Principal intention of a cyber hazard test would be to help in form decision-makers and encourage proper risk answers. Additionally they supply an executive overview to aid executives and supervisors make informed decisions regarding security. The advice security hazard assessment procedure is concerned by answering these questions:

- Which are we's main it resources?
- Exactly what data breach might have a large effect on the business if out of cyber, malware attack or individual mistake? Think consumer info.
- Which will be the important threats and also the hazard sources to your own company?
- Which would be the external and internal vulnerabilities?
- What's the impact if those vulnerabilities are manipulated?
- What's the odds of manipulation?
- What cyber-attacks, cyber dangers, or security episodes can impact affect the potential of the firm to work?
- What's the degree of hazard my company is comfortable carrying?
- Should you Can answer these questions, so you'll have the ability to create a decision of everything to protect. This usually means that you may form IT security controllers and data-security plans to

mitigate hazard. Before it is possible to do this though, you have to answer the next questions:

- what's the risk I'm diminishing?
- Is the maximum priority security hazard?
- Can I reducing the risk at the cheapest way?

This may Help you realize the information value of this data you're attempting to protect and enable you to understand your information hazard management process while in the reach of protecting business requirements.

Why do cyber hazard appraisal?

You will find A range of reasons that you would like to carry out cyber hazard assessment and a couple reasons you want to. Let us walk them through:

- reduction of Long-term prices: identifying possible dangers and vulnerabilities, afterward functioning on equipping them gets got the potential to prevent or reduce safety episodes that saves your company money and/or reputational harm in the Long-term
- Stipulates a cyber protection hazard assessment template for potential examinations: Cyber hazard examinations are not among procedures, You Have

to always update them, performing a Fantastic first flip will probably guarantee favorable processes Despite employees turnover

- better organizational comprehension: Knowing organizational vulnerabilities gives you a clear idea of where your company needs to Boost

- Avoid info breaches: Data breaches may have a massive financial and reputational impact on almost any company

- Avoid regulatory problems: Client information that's stolen as you neglected to comply with HIPAA, Pci-dss or APRA CPS 2 3 4

- Avoid program downtime: Internal or client facing programs Will Need to be accessible and working for both employees and clients to perform their tasks

- Data reduction: Evidence of trade secrets, code, or any other crucial data assets may mean you Shed business to rivals

Beyond This, cyber hazard evaluations are key to Information hazard management and some other company's wider risk management plan.

Who should carry out cyber hazard appraisal?

Ideally Your company has employees in-house that are designed for it. This means using IT staff using a knowledge of how a network and digital infrastructure do the job, in addition to executives that know the way information flows and some other newfound organizational knowledge which might be of good use throughout assessment. Organizational transparency is vital to an intensive cyber hazard appraisal.

Small Organizations might not need the ideal people in-house to execute a comprehensive job and can have to out source examination into an third-party. Businesses are turning into cyber-security computer software to track their cyber-security score, so prevent breaches, send safety surveys and cut back third-party risk.

The best way to Carry out a cyber hazard evaluation

We will Focus on a high level summary and drill down to each measure within the upcoming sections. Before you do any such thing to get started analyzing and mitigating risk, you want to know what data you've got, what infrastructure that you might have, and the financial value of this data you're working to guard. You might choose to begin with auditing your computer data to answer the next questions:

- What data do we collect?
- Just how and where are you currently saving this data?
- Just how can we protect and record the data?
- Just how long do we maintain data?
- Who's access internally and externally into the data?
- Could be your place we're keeping the data correctly procured? Most breaches Result from Badly configured S-3 buckets, assess your S-3 permissions or somebody else will probably

Next, You will wish to specify the parameters of one's own assessment. Below are a number of fantastic primer questions for you started:

- what's the use of the appraisal?
- What's the reach of the appraisal?
- Exist some priorities or limitations that I ought to become conscious of this can impact the appraisal?
- Who would I want use of at the company to receive all of the advice I desire?
- What hazard model does the company use for hazard investigation?

A Great Deal of These queries are self explanatory. What you truly want to understand is what you will be studying, with got the expertise needed to precisely assess, and also therefore are there some regulatory requirements or funding limitations that you want to be conscious of.

Now let us Look at exactly what steps will need to be studied to finish a comprehensive cyber hazard assessment, giving you a hazard assessment template.

Many Organizations do not possess an infinite funding for information hazard management therefore that it's ideal to limit your range to the maximum up-to-date assets.

To save Time and money after, spend time specifying a benchmark for discovering the most crucial of the advantage. Most businesses include strength value, legal status and company importance. Once the benchmark is officially incorporated into the company's information hazard management policy, then utilize it to categorize each advantage as critical, major or minor.

You will find Many questions that you may ask to find out appreciate:

- is there any legal or financial penalties related to losing or exposing this info?
- Just how valuable is the information into a rival?
- Can we recreate that this advice from scrape? How long could it take and what could be the associated costs?
- Want losing this advice impact on earnings or earnings?
- Want losing this data impact daily small business surgeries? Can our staff work with no?
- What is that the reputational damage with the data getting leaked?

Measure Two: Describe and prioritize resources

The Very First Step would be to recognize resources to both appraise and determine the reach of the appraisal. This will let you prioritize which resources to check. You could not need to carry out an appraisal on every construction, employee, email data, trade secret, vehicle, and also part of office equipment. Bear in mind not all resources have the same price.

You Require To operate with business management and users to make a set of valuable assets. For every asset, collect the following information where relevant:

- Computer Software
- Hardware
- Data
- Interface
- End users
- Support private
- Purpose
- Criticality
- Functional demands
- IT safety policies
- IT security structure
- Network topology
- data storage security
- Information-flow
- Technical safety controllers
- Physical safety controllers
- Environmental safety

A danger Is any vulnerability which would possibly be exploited to breach security to create injury or steal data out of the own organization. While malware, hackers, as well as other IT security risks jump to mind, you'll find lots of different dangers:

- Natural disasters: Floods, hurricanes, earthquakes, lightning and flame may destroy as far as any cyber offender. You can't just lose servers but servers too.

When picking between on premise and cloud-based servers, then take into consideration the opportunity of natural disasters.

- System collapse: Are you currently critical systems ranning on high-tech gear? Can they have good service?

- Human mistake: Why are your S-3 buckets holding sensitive information precisely configured? Does your firm have appropriate instruction across malware, phishing along with societal technology? Anybody can unintentionally click on a malware connection or input their credentials to some phishing scam. You have to possess strong IT security controllers for example routine data backups, password managers, etc..

- Adversarial risks: Third-party sellers, insiders, reliable insiders, privileged insiders, based hacker collectives, Random classes, corporate espionage, providers, Nationstates.

Some Frequent dangers that impact every company include:

- Unauthorized access: either by attackers malware, employee mistake

- Misuse of information by licensed users: normally a cyber hazard where data is changed, deleted or employed without any consent

- Data flows: permanently identifiable information (PII) as well as also other sensitive data by Investors or through poor arrangement of CloudServices

- loss in data: company falls or inadvertently deleted data as a piece of very poor backup or replication

- Service disturbance: lack in revenue or reputational damage caused by downtime

- Later You've identified the dangers confronting your company, you will need to estimate your own impact.

Today it is Time to go from everything "can" eventually what's a possibility of happening. A vulnerability is a weakness a hazard could use to breach security, injury your own organization, or steal sensitive data. Vulnerabilities are observed through exposure investigation, audit reports, and the National Institute for Standards and Technology (NIST) vulnerability database, seller data, incident reply teams, along with computer software security investigation.

You are able to Reduce organizational software-based vulnerabilities with good patch direction via automatic driven upgrades. But remember physical vulnerabilities, the prospect of some one gaining access to a business's computing process is significantly paid off insurance firm's key card access.

Analyze Controls in place to reduce or remove the chances of vulnerability or threat. Controls may be put into place through technical methods, such as applications or applications, encryption, intrusion detection mechanics, two-factor authentication, automatic upgrades, continuous data flow detection or through non-technical methods such as security policies and physiological mechanics like locks or key card access.

Controls Must be categorized like preventative or detective controllers. Preventative controls try to avoid attacks such as encryption, anti-virus or continuous security tracking, detective controls decide to try to detect as soon as an attack has happened like continuous data vulnerability detection.

Now you Understand the advice value, risks, vulnerabilities and controllers, another action is to spot the way likely those cyber threats will be that occurs and their impact should they happen. It isn't merely whether you may possibly face these events sooner or later, however what it's prospect of success might be.

Imagine You own a database which save all of your organization's most sensitive data and this advice is appreciated by $100 million based on your own quotes.

Now you Estimate that in case of a violation, at least 1 / 2 your data could be subjected before it could be contained. This leads to an estimated loss of $50 million. However, you hope that is not likely that occurs, state a one in annually occurrence. Leading to an estimated loss of 50m every 50 decades or at annual provisions, $1 million each year.

Potentially Justifying a $ 1million funding annually to be averted.

Utilize danger Degree for being a basis and determine activities for senior management or other responsible people to mitigate the chance. Here are some basic tips:

- Non - corrective steps to be created when you can
- Moderate - proper measures developed over a reasonable Time Period
- Non - determine whether to take the hazard or mitigate

- Bear in Mind, You've determined the worth of this advantage along with how much you really may pay to protect it. The second phase is easy: When it costs to guard the advantage than it's worthwhile, perhaps it doesn't sound right to make use of a preventative controller to protect it. Nevertheless, remember that there might possibly be reputational effect perhaps not merely financial impact therefore it's necessary to factor that intoo.

Additionally Consider:

- Organizational policies
- Reputational damage
- Feasibility
- Regulations
- Impact of controllers
- Security
- Reliability
- hierarchical mindset towards hazard
- Tolerance for doubt regarding hazard factors
- Organizational weighting of risk factors

The closing Step is always to build up a hazard assessment report to encourage direction in making decision in funding, policies and procedures. For every hazard, the report should clarify the risk, vulnerabilities and value. Together side the impact and probability of occurrence and control tips.

As you Work by means of this procedure, you are going to know what infrastructure your organization functions, what exactly your valuable data will be, and the way you are able to better secure and operate your enterprise. After that you can create a hazard assessment policy which defines exactly what your company need to do occasionally to track its security position, the risks are addressed and mitigated, and the way you may perform another risk assessment procedure.

Whether or not You're your little business or multinational enterprise information hazard management is at the center of cyber-security. These procedures help set guidelines and rules which provide responses from what dangers and vulnerabilities could lead to financial and reputational injury to your small business and also the way they're mitigated.

Ideally, As your safety implementations improve and also you answer the contents of one's present assessment, your cyber-security score should change.

The best way to Carry out a cyber hazard evaluation

Every Company desires a cyber hazard evaluation now, here is what you want to understand. A cyber hazard assessment can be a essential part of a organization or company's risk management plan. Now, pretty much every company is based on it and data systems to ran business. Risks up until the digital era, the employers never had to essentially cope with.

Risk Evaluations are not anything fresh. They will have been with us in some form or another since the early Egyptians, once they'd use many calculations to attempt to determine if or not they had to store extra grain up as the Nile river could don't flooding. For all intents and purposes, they turned into more formalized from early 1900s when labor moves started pushing for safer workplace requirements. And also you need to take care once you are searching for information about performing a cyber hazard investigation, since in the event that you forget that the word "cyber" you wind up in a property of industrial manufacturing injuries and death and dismemberment clauses.

That is The reason why we've come up with this guide about the best way best to carry out proper cyber hazard appraisal. We'll be moving by National Institute of Standards and Technology (NIST) Tips. NIST is really a US agency that has wrapped up beneath the Department of Commerce. It provides assistance with matters such as encryption best techniques. When you'll notice, in addition, it provides something for calculating hazard which is going to be of good use even as we develop our analytics.

Why take a cyber-security hazard appraisal?

Risk evaluation -- the procedure of identifying, analysing and Evaluating hazard -- would be the only means to make certain the cyber-security controllers you select work to the risks that the organization faces.

With no hazard appraisal to notify your cyber safety Choices, you might spend time, energy and tools. There's very little point executing measures to shield against events which will probably not occur or will not impact your business enterprise.

Likewise, It's likely You Will underestimate or Overlook dangers which might lead to substantial damage. This is the reason why so many best practice frameworks, laws and standards -- for example, GDPR (General data-protection

Legislation) along with DPA (Data Protection Act) 2018 --
require hazard evaluations should be conducted.

Exactly what exactly does a cyber-security hazard
assessment demand?

A cyber safety hazard assessment describes the a Variety of
Details Assets which would possibly be suffering from a
cyberattack (for instance, systems, hardware, laptops,
customer data and intellectual property), after which
explains the numerous risks which may influence those
resources.

A hazard estimate and analytics are often done, Followed
with the variety of controls to take care of the specified
risks.

It's important to constantly monitor and examine the threat
Environment to discover some changes from the
circumstance of this business enterprise, and also to
maintain an summary of the comprehensive hazard
management procedure.

ISO 27001 and cyber dangers

The global Conventional ISO/IEC 27001:2013 (ISO 27001)
provides the criteria for a best practice ISMS (information
security management platform) -- a risk-based method of

information security risk management that covers people, technology and processes.

Clause 6.1.2 of those conventional sets from the needs of The data security risk assessment procedure. Organizations must:

Establish and maintain certain information security hazard standards.

Make sure that repeated hazard examinations "produce consistent, valid and similar outcomes."

Describe"risks connected to the increased loss in confidentiality, integrity and accessibility for advice within the range of the data security management strategy" and establish the proprietors of these risks.

Analyse and appraise information security risks, in accordance with the criteria shown sooner.

It's important that businesses"maintain documented Information concerning the data security risk assessment process" in order they are able to demonstrate they conform to all these conditions.

Additionally they will have to follow a number of measures -- and Create relevant documentation as a portion of this information security hazard treatment procedure.

ISO 27005 offers tips for data security threat Evaluations and is intended to help with the execution of a risk-based ISMS.

IT Governance hazard assessment services

Assessing a cyber safety hazard assessment without specialist Guidance is just a intricate procedure which requires significant preparation, specialist knowledge and stake holder buyin.

Save time and prevent error and trial using IT Governance's Range of risk investigation and cyber-security services and products.

Risks presented by the Cyber-security threat landscape are Increasingly section of this ERM equation, and this introduces a struggle for CISOs along with different senior security professionals. Quantifying the company impact of a cyber-security event is just a rather hard, maybe hopeless job, and measuring the reality of such a conference is much tougher.

Enterprise risk management Procedure

Many organizations are doing this. In Aetna, for Instance, Cyber-security risks are thought a portion of operational risk at the organization's enterprise risk management frame. These risks are qualitative and specific. In reality, there exists a regular risk score which gets fed into the ERM system.

CSO Jim Routh is Not Just accountable for this particular procedure, but Is additionally an associate of this hazard committee that offers government for Aetna's ERM program. "Safety is increasing insignificance to successful business operational risk management," he states. "Tight orientation with ERM and emergency management programs is crucial."

Security is growing in importance to successful enterprise Operational threat managementTight orientation with ERM and emergency management programs is vital.

It is not enough to go by financing requirements, Routh adds. "The rapid development of hazard celebrity plans requires constant growth of control design and efficacy," he states. "Regulatory compliance is crucial, however, insufficient to attain venture resiliency."
Emphasizing business impact is Another way to consider About cyber-security, also it needs a different mindset compared to the responding to cyber-security dangers.

Cyber-security was about averting strikes, and also a violation either happened or it did not.

"Today, most organizations know that Cyber-security Is perhaps not really a challenge to be resolved but also a probability to be handled," says Andrew Morrison, pioneer of plan shield and answer for cyber hazard services at Deloitte & Touche. "Many of this current market is acclimated to the simple fact it's no longer in case an attack will probably occur and the way that we'll manage it. That entails a entirely different mindset. "Hazards, naturally, could be taken, falsified, or moved," he states.

Nowadays, most organizations know that Cyber-security Isn't A difficulty to be solved however, also a probability to be handled.

ERM frameworks

There is often a disconnect between the speech of safety And the terminology of risk, which may make it tougher for a CSO to engage in a meaningful part in the venture risk management conversation. In reality, lots of cyber-security pros throw their hands up in amazement when asked concerning how they measure the risk reduction correlated with particular reduction plans, and instead indicate websites reports regarding breaches, cyber-security frameworks such as NIST and FAIR, or even usable metrics if asked for empowerment.

Back in ERM frameworks, the term "danger" Has a really Particular significance. Cyber-security leaders that show up from the other hand, since many do, often tend to concentrate on very strategic technical problems, as opposed to bottom-line impacts. By way of instance, if a vulnerability is not calibrated, there exists a risk that attackers may use it to steal data.

A business-focused outline of exactly the same difficulty, But may possibly be the minding the vulnerability will cut the probability of a violation to a certain database, and that, if exposed, will probably surely cost a specific number of money in lost business, penalties and remediation expenses. Now, the business may find out if or not a reduction program would make bottom-line feel or in the event the decrease in hazard isn't significant, or so the database isn't significant enough, and the business is way better off hanging out and money else where.

According to some experts, that really isn't possible. "There is no means of calculating how far the execution of each control reduces the risk," says Matt McBride, EVP for digital transformation in Genesis10, which assists businesses develop plans to deal with cyber-security problems like patch direction.

Alternatively, McBride says, he assists businesses mitigate dangers Based on exactly what the largest dangers are. "But we aren't quantifying the particular shift in risk in line with executing a specific tool or application. We can chat about moving a company out of a high-ranking position to your medium-risk position to your low-risk posture"

No Cyber-security frame will measure the economic Price That outcomes, but McBride claims. "In my own experience, businesses do not speak about a specific significance for reducing danger.

Rather than discussing potential dangers, Cyber-security Professionals often attempt to market a narrative for their own board to warrant the budgets. "They have captured in hurling FUD around," says Brian Reed, analyst at Gartner, Inc."Everybody knows that there are frightful stories available to frighten you"

It is the right time to quit scaring fearful men and women, Reed states. "The next problem is if cyber-security technologists enter the front of board members and senior management they give attention to lots of geeky coolness," he states. "it is too little communication between technical persons and people. It's precisely the very same problem we've ever needed. Business people do not know technology complications, and tech people do not understand just how exactly to establish business worth"

Thus, as an Example, a CSO moving facing senior administration To chat about resources could turn into news headlines being a crutch, like a huge brand new vulnerability that influenced other businesses, being a chance to delve deeper into technical specifics and create a few emotional effects. "did something happen in the news headlines?" Says Matt Wilson, Chief Information Security Advisor in Pennsylvania-based consulting firm BTB Security. "Can it induce folks to strike us"

Should they attempt and put a risk-related amount onto it, then it is quite Subjective, Wilson states. "They will put some recommendations concerning what each number means, however they truly are really made up if folks are scoring it out. It's similar to financial trades, where they could calculate percent of fraud, that will be really a somewhat straightforward metric that is around 50, 60 decades or longer"

Dion Lisle, leader at the Same World Identity, a San Francisco-based cyber-security consulting business, says he's not yet met anybody who is solved the issue of calculating cyber-security hazard. "Many ERM frameworks are constructed round the famous topics," he states. "There are no known difficulties in this particular space. Every event was unprecedented. Just how will you calculate unprecedented hazard"

Alternatively, CSOs are concentrated on functional issues, for example Reducing prices, "he says. If it is the right time to rate hazard to gauge the effectiveness of these security apps, they turn into anecdotes. "Goal had a violation, therefore needed a violation, fifty-million users are subjected on facebook," Lisle states. "But no body really is at the idea of view, 'That really is really a 40 million risk and that I need $10 million to correct it.' I have not heard that dialog out of anybody I understand. There are not enough data points to compute it"

It'll take a change from the tactical to a strategic Mindset, he says, also increasing collaboration between financial actuarial pros and technologists, Lisle states. "I presume that it's really a fresh subject, where IT and fund must meet up and organize."

Quantifying Cyber-security hazard an uncertain science
Wilson and Lisle are not the ones stating that it is overly
Ancient to put hard numbers on cyber-security risks. "The
very major insurance companies now aren't widely boosting
cyber insurance policy policies," says Nathan Wenzler, chief
security strategist in AsTech. "They exist, and they are
becoming more of something, but there isn't any static data
that is consistent across the board"

Think about sellers claiming hazard scorecards? "Inside my
Opinion, it's mostly hype," Wenzler states. "Trainers that
correct their score-card do not frequently discuss the
simple fact it is time intensive to ascertain the risk factors
and classify all of the resources and organize it and record it
so you may then feed it to these processes"

Artificial intelligence (AI) and machine learning might
assist, Nonetheless it requires human investigation to
create the final conclusions -- which is plenty of hard labor.
But for several businesses, the campaign pays off. "Several
businesses have been identified criticality levels for many
their sections and data, plus they truly are at a better place
to find automatic coverage out-of-it to receive their single
pane of glass in their hazard," Wenzler states. "However, if
you desire to have that opinion, it is really a whole lot of

work. I consult a number of businesses with this sort of item, and many do not done this."

To create useful diagrams and scores, companies have to Classify every advantage, for example data, and also the functions they play at the provider, and also the significance of these business purposes and data, Wenzler states. "When you've completed most that legwork, and assemble most that info, then you're able to put it in your ERM system that'll cranch all that down data and supply you with a scorecard."

A Growing Number of CSOs have been asked to Do Precisely That, states Jon Oltsik, senior chief analyst at Enterprise Strategy Group. "There is a transition happening" The hazard amounts are quotes, which is tough to find the proper statistics and also make the ideal evaluations, he says, however, CSOs are determining how to doit. "That is what the company people wish to watch," he states.

Cyber-security does possess any special challenges, such as Third-party black and risks swan events, however, that happens in different fields of business, too, states Jim Reavis, CEO in Cloud Security Alliance. "There is probably a level to that it's more inconsistent," he states. "But we've got a whole lot of information on the market, and also a great deal of businesses are dedicated to this "

The Increase of the cyber protection industry is 1 case of The way cyber-security risk will be calculated," states jordan, senior manager at Santa Fe Group, a consulting business which helps businesses appraise third-party vendors. "They have got a reasonably good idea about what it is that they're prepared to insure and also the security measures they might require you have set up so as to acquire yourself a policy," he states. Additionally, there are vendors which could quantify a business's hazard from the exterior, searching for vulnerable systems, and analytics companies that'll ran cyber-security audits. "It is becoming more art, and more mathematics," he states.

The best way to Figure the Influence of your Cyber-security occasion

Business effect Could Be the first Half this Cyber-security risk Equation, also certainly will be the simplest part, specially for large businesses. "In Fortune 500 organizations, there usually are ERM apps already in position," says John Pescatore, manager of emerging trends at SANS Institute. "it is an essential starting place. The company concentrate on hazard is usually pretty much recognized for any provider that is been in operation for a little while."

Nevertheless, that the Cyber-security facets May Not function Based, Pescatore adds, also this is a location where CSOs need to work with sections. As an instance, he says, fed ex is accustomed to planning such as threats of disruptions that happen around Christmas, as it is a busy season to your own delivery company. Back in 2017, though, a ransom-ware attack struck in June and also did around $300 million worth of damage. "That happened in their mind," he states. "However these certainly weren't utilized to considering this "

Regulated businesses have compliance frameworks which may Help identify areas where cyber-security strikes might have a direct effect, for example as PCI from the retail industry, HIPAA in healthcare, and the numerous frameworks that are pertinent to financial firms, publicly traded businesses, and government builders, however they truly are only a starting place, " says Pescatore.

Require PCI, for instance. The Payment Card Industry Security Standards Council targets protecting credit card info. A ransom-ware attack which chooses cash registers offline may not demand a data breach but can still bring about a business significant financial annoyance. "it mightn't be considered a PCI dilemma because no data will be vulnerable, but earnings goes down, and also the traces could get more, and it'd have been a key monetary impact," Pescatore says.

Finding critical business process that may be affected By cyber-security events is actually a very important endeavor, but many are unsuccessful, Pescatore says. "Lots of CSOs aren't knowledgeable enough by that which exactly is vital to the business enterprise and also have yet to be success at this"

The best way to Compute the likelihood of a Cyber-security occasion

Calculating the Possible Effect of the event addresses Just 1 / 2 of this hazard equation, nevertheless. To figure out the possibility of an episode can be an equally tough job.

Sovos Compliance, which helps businesses with their taxation And funding requirements, has handled this issue using an outside-in strategy. CSO John Strasser came into the company five years ago specifically to launch an information security program for your whole company, and also the infosec ERM process has paved the way for the remaining portion of the business, he states.

It's absolutely possible to calculate the danger a Special vulnerability or alternative security dilemma may lead to damage to your provider, Strasser claims. "I really say that unquestionably, but also with a little bit of understanding there is a degree of qualitative and hierarchical agreement the business has to utilize."

Strasser sits with all the Corporation's CEO and CTO Atleast Once annually also determines the hazard values for the impact and the odds of cyber-security events. "From that point, you are able to execute a variety of calculations," he states. "You are able to turn into specific metrics which induce the true hazard down scores, and that means you're able to track your overall hazard posture as time passes. It can help supply a whole lot of clarity at the activities you require."

The initial 1 / 2 of this hazard calculation, the effect, is Predicated on the indirect and direct costs on the company of a conference, like losing a data center or some pair of data. Afterward, to figure out the chance of an occasion, there exists a composite of general data, internal input signal, and outside testing. By way of instance, with an info center, a corporation is able to start looking at publicly available details on the subject of the frequency in which fires and earthquakes occur.

That data is more difficult to locate for cyber-attacks. For these Amounts, Sovos uses third-party immersion testers to gauge how simple it is to get some one to break into the systems -- even the longer hours it will take, and also the greater the degree of skill demanded, the low the odds that the attack could succeed.

"I do not believe anybody has a magic bullet into estimating Efficacy of controllers," Strasser says. "What we have been left with is constant testing of those controllers, together with exposure red and scanning team-blue team and higher level penetration testing"

When can boards prevent fretting about cyber-attacks? Cyber-security dangers are bothersome for corporate boards, says Dan Kinsella, partner at Deloitte Risk and Financial Advisory. "I keep intouch with boards regularly onto this issue," he states.

Before, a threat could Appear prior to the board the Company should think of a strategy to manage it, also it's really completed. "The Topics was addressed the board has to discuss it." For Instance, If there is a danger of a passion, a Business might Choose to set up Sprinklers and purchase fire protection.

CHAPTER SEVEN
SOCIAL ENGINEERING

Social engineering is the art of manipulating individuals so that they Give up confidential details. The kinds of advice these offenders are searching could vary, however if folks are targeted that the offenders usually are hoping to fool you into providing them with all your passwords or bank info, or get your own pc to covertly install malicious applications --that'll let them have use of your own passwords and bank information in addition to giving control on your PC.

Criminals utilize social networking strategies because It's usually More straightforward to exploit the natural tendency to anticipate than it really is to find strategies to hack on your applications. By way of instance, it's far simpler to fool somebody into giving you their password than it's for one to try out hacking on their password (unless your password is very feeble).

Security is about knowing and what to anticipate. It Really Is Crucial to understand when and when to not choose someone in their sentence so when the individual who you are communicating with is that they say they truly are. The same goes of internet connections and website usage: if do you hope that the website you're using is valid or is definitely safe to offer your advice?

Ask any safety practitioner and They'll tell you that the Weakest link in the security series is the individual who takes a individual or scenario in mind value. It is irrelevant exactly how many locks and dead bolts are in your own doors and doors, or should have protect dogs, alert systems, flood lights, fences with barbed wire, and armed security employees; if you expect that the individual at the gate that says that could be your pizza delivery guy and you let him without checking to see whether he's valid you're completely vulnerable to anything risk he symbolizes.

What Can a Social Engineering Attack Seem like?

Mail from a buddy
In case a criminal succeeds to hack on or socially engineer a single individual's Email password that they will have use of this individual's contact list--because most men and women utilize a password anywhere they probably have use of this individual's social media contacts too.

Once the offender has that email accounts under their hands, They send mails to all anyone's contacts leave messages all their close friend's societal pages, and on the pages of their friend's friends.

Taking good advantage of your own confidence and fascination, these messages may:

· Contain a Hyperlink Which You have to See --and as the connection comes from the buddy and you are interested, you'll expect that the connection and then click on and be infected with malware therefore the offender can take over your device and also accumulate your own contacts information and also fool them like you had been scammed

· Include a downloading of music, pictures, picture, record, etc., which contains malicious applications embedded. In the event you download -- that you're very likely to do because you imagine it really is from the friend -- you eventually become infected. The offender has access to a system, email accounts, societal networking accounts and accounts, and also the attack propagates to everybody you understand. On, and forth.

Mail from a different reliable origin

Phishing Strikes certainly are a sub set of social technologies plan that imitate a trusted origin and concoct a seemingly plausible scenario for handing login credentials or other sensitive private information. As stated by Webroot statistics, finance institutions represent the great most impersonated businesses as well as in accordance with Verizon's annual Data Breach Investigations Report, social engineering attacks involving phishing and pretexting (see below) are accountable for 93 percent of powerful data breaches.

Working with a persuasive story or pretext, these messages can:

· Urgently request the help. They require one to send money in order that they may secure home and so they inform you how you can send the cash into the offender.

· Use phishing efforts having a legitimate-seeming desktop. Ordinarily, a phisher sends an email, IM, opinion, or text that appears to result from a valid, favorite corporation, bank, school, or association.

· Request you to subscribe with their own charitable fund raiser, or another cause. Probably with guidelines about what best to send the dollars to this offender. Preying on kindness and kindness, these phishers request assistance or service for any disaster, political effort, or even charity is top-of-mind.

·The hyperlink location might seem really legitimate together with most of the ideal logos, and articles (in reality, the offenders might have reproduced the specific arrangement and content of their valid site). Because every thing appears plausible, you hope that the email and also the counterfeit site and furnish whatever advice that the crook is requesting for. All these sorts of phishing scams frequently feature a warning of what's going to occur in the event that you neglect to do something soon because offenders understand that should they are able to get one to behave before you believe you are much more inclined to fall due to their phishing effort.

· Informs you that you're a 'winner' Perhaps the email claims to be out of the lottery, or even a deceased relative, or even perhaps the millionth person to select their website, etc.. As a way to provide you with the 'winnings' you need to give info regarding your bank routing so that they understand just how to send it for you or provide your address and contact number in order that they may send the trophy, and you also can also be requested to prove that you might be frequently involving your social security number. All these would be the 'greed phishes' where if the narrative pre-text is sparse, folks need what can be acquired and collapse to get it giving their advice, then using their bank accounts emptied, and also individuality stolen.

· Acts as a supervisor or coworker. It may possibly request a upgrade in an crucial, proprietary job your company is now focusing , for payment advice regarding a business charge card, or another query masquerading as daily business enterprise.

Baiting situations

These societal technologies schemes understand that in Case You dangle Something people need, a lot of men and women would choose the lure. These strategies are frequently entirely on peer-to-peer internet sites that provides a download of something similar to a sexy brand new picture, or even music. However, the strategies are also entirely on social media websites, malicious internet sites you see search benefits, etc.

Or, the strategy may appear as a remarkably Fantastic bargain on Classified websites, auction websites, etc.. To allay your feeling, you may observe the seller really has a fantastic rating (all intended and crafted beforehand time).

Individuals who take the lure could be infected with malicious applications That could generate numerous fresh loopholes against their contacts, can lose their money without receiving their purchased thing, also even when these were idiotic enough to cover a test, may possibly find their banking accounts vacant.

Answer to some query you had
Criminals may feign to be reacting to your pursuit for Help' out of an organization whilst at the same time offering more assistance. They pick businesses that huge numbers of individuals use like an applications corporation or bank. If you never utilize the service or product, you'll dismiss the email, call, or message, but when you do have been using the service, then there's just a fantastic chance that you will respond as you almost certainly do need help with an issue.

By Way of Example, Though you know you did not initially ask a Question you likely an issue with your personal computer's operating system and also you grab on this chance to receive it fixed. At no cost! The instant that you respond you've obtained the crook's narrative, awarded them your confidence and put up yourself for manipulation.

The agent, Who's really a criminal, will probably want to 'authenticate you', possess you loginto 'their machine' or, maybe you have login your computer system and give them remote access for a computer so that they are able to 'fix' it to you, or inform you that the controls which means that you may fix it your self together with their assistance -- where a number of the orders they let you input will soon open a method for your offender to get into your computer after.

Creating hindsight

Some societal technology, is about producing disbelief, or Starting battles; those tend to be completed by people that you understand and that are mad with you personally, however it's also achieved by nasty individuals only attempting to wreak havoc, even individuals who desire to create disbelief in the mind others in order that they are able to then measure into as a fanatic and also attain your confidence, or from extortionists who need to manipulate advice and threaten you with sin.

This form of social technology frequently begins by gaining entry Into a message accounts or a different communicating accounts in an IM client, societal networking, chat, forum, etc.. They accomplish that by hacking, social engineering, or even simply just imagining very weak passwords.

· The malicious person might then alter private or sensitive communications (like graphics and sound) with basic editing methods and forward these to additional folks to make play, uncertainty, humiliation, etc.. They can allow it to seem as if it had been unintentionally delivered, or appear as they have been allowing you to realize what's' ally' moving on.

· Instead they can utilize the modified material to make money from anyone they hacked or by the assumed receiver.

There are literally thousands of variants to societal Engineering strikes. The only real limitation to the amount of ways they are able to subconsciously users by means of this sort of harness would be your offender's imagination. And also you will experience numerous kinds of exploits in one attack. Afterward your offender is very likely to offer your advice to the others so that they also can conduct their exploits against you personally, your associates, your friends' friends, and etc as offenders leverage people's lost confidence.

Do not become a victim

While cyber-attacks are uncontrolled, short-lived, and require just a Couple users to select the lure for a fruitful effort, you can find ways for protecting your self. Most do not require far more than paying attention to the important points before you personally. Continue to keep these in mind in order to avoid getting phished your self.

Ideas to Understand:

· Melts down. Spammers would like you to do something first and think later. In the event the message communicates a feeling of urgency or utilizes high-income sales approaches be cynical; not make their urgency influence your careful inspection.

· Research the truth . Be skeptical of any messages that are unsolicited. When the email looks like it's out of an organization that you employ, do your research. Use an internet search engine to visit the actual company's site, or even perhaps a telephone directory to discover their contact number.

· Do not let a connection be accountable for where you property. Stay accountable for locating the internet site your self with an internet search engine to make certain that you property where you want to land. Hovering more links in email will demonstrate the true URL at the end, however a fantastic imitation may still steer you wrong.

· Email hi-jacking is uncontrolled. Hackers, spammers, along with societal engineers carrying control of individuals email accounts (along with other communicating reports) is becoming uncontrolled. Once they restrain a message accounts, they prey to the confidence of their individual's contacts. Even if the sender seems to be some one who you know, in the event that you're not expecting a message with a connection or attachment test together with your friend before launching downloading or links.

· Beware of any download. In case you do not recognize the sender AND expect a document from their store, downloading whatever is an error.

· Foreign deals are imitation. In the event you get a contact from an overseas lottery or sweepstakes or money in an unknown relative, or asks to move funds from an overseas country to get a share of this amount of money it's certainto become a scam.

Approaches to Protect Your Self:

· Delete any petition financial data or passwords. In the event you receive asked to respond to a note together with private info, it is really a scam.

· Reject asks for assistance or supplies of assistance. Legitimate businesses and associations usually do not contact you to give assist. If you didn't expressly ask the aid of the sender, then consider any deal to 'help' renew fico ratings, refinance a house, answer the question, etc., some scam. In the same way, in case you get a petition help from the charity or company you usually do not need a relationship together, then delete it. To contribute, search out reputable charitable businesses in your to prevent falling for a scam.

· Establish your spam blockers into high. Every email application contains spam blockers. For starters, examine your preferences options, and place them -- only make sure you look at your spam folder occasionally to see whether valid email was trapped. You might even hunt for a detail by detail guide to setting your spam blockers by simply hunting in the name of your email provider in addition to the word's pam filters'.

· Safe your calculating apparatus. Install anti-virus applications, firewalls, email filters and also maintain those uptodate. Establish your os to automatically upgrade, of course when your own smartphone will not automatically upgrade, manually upgrade it once you are given a note to accomplish that. Use an AntiPhishing tool provided by your internet browser or alternative party to alert one to risks.

Webroot's hazard database includes over 600 million domain names and 27 billion URLs classified to shield users against threats that were on-line. The hazard intelligence financing most our services and products makes it possible to employ the web firmly, and also our cellphone security solutions offer secure web surfing to stop malware attacks that are successful.

Social engineering is the art of manipulating individuals They stop trying confidential details. The kinds of advice these offenders are searching could vary, however if folks are targeted that the offenders are often hoping to fool you into providing them with all your passwords or bank info, or get your own pc to covertly install malicious applications -- that'll let them have use of your own passwords and bank information in addition to giving control on your PC.

Criminals utilize social networking strategies as It is Usually less difficult to use your natural tendency to anticipate than it really is to find strategies to hack on your applications. By way of instance, it's far simpler to fool somebody into giving you their password than it's for one to try out hacking on their password (unless your password is very feeble).

Security is about knowing and what to anticipate. It Really Is Crucial to understand when and when to not choose someone in their sentence so when the individual who you are communicating with is that they say they truly are. The same goes of internet connections and website usage: if do you hope that the website you're using is valid or is definitely safe to offer your advice?

Ask any safety practitioner and They'll tell you the The weakest link in the security series is that the individual who takes a man or woman or scenario in mind value. It is irrelevant exactly how many locks and dead bolts are in your own doors and doors, or should have protect dogs, alert systems, flood lights, fences with barbed wire, and armed security employees; if you expect that the individual at the gate that says that could be your pizza delivery guy and you let him without checking to see whether he's valid you're completely vulnerable to anything risk he symbolizes.

Ideas to Understand:

· Slow-down. Spammers would like you to do something first and think later. In the event the message communicates a feeling of urgency or utilizes high-income earnings approaches be cynical; not make their urgency influence your careful inspection.

· Research the truth. Be skeptical of any messages that are unsolicited. When the email looks like it's out of an organization that you employ, do your research. Use an internet search engine to visit the actual company's site, or even perhaps a telephone directory to discover their contact number.

· Do not let a connection be accountable for where you property. Remain in control by locating the internet site your self with an internet search engine to make certain that you property where you want to land. Hovering more links in email will demonstrate the true URL in the floor, but a fantastic imitation can still steer you wrong.

· Email hi-jacking is uncontrolled. Hackers, spammers, along with societal engineers carrying control of individuals email accounts (along with other communicating reports) is becoming uncontrolled. Once they restrain a message accounts, they prey to the confidence of their individual's contacts. Even if the sender seems to be some one who you know, in the event that you're not expecting a message with an associate or attachment test together with your friend before opening downloading or links.

· Watch out for any download. In case you do not recognize the sender AND expect a document from these, downloading whatever is a blunder.

· Foreign deals are imitation. In the event you get a contact from an overseas lottery or sweepstakes or money in an unknown relative, or asks to move funds from an overseas country to get a share of this amount of money it's certainto become a scam.

SORTS OF SOCIAL ENGINEERING STRIKES

Popular forms of social engineering attacks comprise:

- Baiting: Baiting is if An individual leaves a malware-infected mechanical apparatus, like being a USB flash Drive, where it's guaranteed to be found. The finder picks up the Apparatus and loads it on their computer, inadvertently installing The malware.

- Phishing: Phishing is when a malicious party sends a deceptive email disguised as a Legitimate email, frequently purporting to be from the trusted source. The Message is supposed to deceive the receiver into sharing financial or personal Clicking or information onto a connection which supports malware.

- Spear-phishing: Spear-phishing is similar to phishing but tailored for a Particular person or organization.

- Vishing: Vishing can also be Called voice Phishing, also it has the usage of social technology within the Phone to collect financial and personal information from the prospective.

- Pretexting: Pretexting is if one celebration is present to another to access privileged data. By Way of Example, a pretexting scam may call for an attacker that pretends To want financial or personal data so as to validate the identity of this recipient.

- Scareware: Scareware entails Tricking the victim to believing that the computer system is infected with malware Has accidentally downloaded prohibited content. The attacker subsequently supplies the Victim a remedy which may correct the fake problem; the truth is, the victim Is simply duped into downloading and installing the attacker's malware.

- Water-holing: A watering Hole assault is once the attacker tries to undermine a certain Group of individuals by infecting internet sites they're known to trust and visit in Order to obtain access.

- Diversion thieving: In this specific Type of assault, the societal specialists suggestion that a courier or delivery company Right into visiting the incorrect pickup or dropoff location, therefore diluting the Trade.

- Quid-pro-quo: A Quid-pro Quo strike is one by the societal scientist dared to supply Something beforehand for the mark's advice or assistance. To get Example, a hacker calls for a choice of random numbers inside an Company and thought to be calling back from tech service. Finally, the hacker will probably locate somebody with a valid technician dilemma that They will subsequently feign to provide help. Through this, the consumer could possess the Target kind from the controls to establish malware or may amass password information.

- Honey snare: An assault in That your societal scientist must be a stylish person to socialize With a individual on the web, pretend an online relationship and gather sensitive Advice throughout that relationship.

- Tail Gating: Tail-gating, occasionally known as Piggy Backing, Is each time a hacker walks right into a bonded construction by abiding by somebody with An access card that is authorized. This assault supposes the Individual with valid Access into this construction is considerate enough to contain the door open to your own Man supporting them, presuming they have been allowed to function there.

- Rogue: Rogue security applications is a Kind of malware That tips aims into paying to get your own imitation elimination of malware.

Cases of social engineering Strikes

Perhaps the Most Well-known social engineering strike comes From the mythical Trojan War by that the Greeks could actually be into the city of Troy and win against the war by hiding in a huge wooden horse which has been presented towards the Trojan army for being a gift of calmness.

Frank Abagnale is considered among the leading specialists in Social technology methods. From the 1960s, he used many approaches to impersonate at eight people, including an airline pilot, a doctor and a lawyer. Abagnale was likewise a test forger in this moment. After his incarceration he became a security consultant for the FBI and started their or her own monetary fraud consultancy. His adventures as a youthful optimism guy were made famous because of their own bestselling novel Catch Me If You Can and the picture adaptation out of Oscar-winning manager Steven Spielberg.

A newer example of an effective social technology Attack was that the 2011 data violation of security company RSA. A attacker delivered two separate emails over two weeks to small categories of RSA employees. The mails had the subject line"2011 Recruitment Strategy" and included an Excel file attachment. The dictionary included malicious code which installed a back door through an Adobe Flash vulnerability. While it wasn't clarified what information had been stolen, when any, RSA's SecurID two-factor authentication (2FA) strategy was endangered, and also the organization spent approximately $66 million recovering against the attack.

In 2013, the Syrian Electronics Army managed to get the Associated Press' Twitter accounts by adding a malicious link in a malicious email address. The email had been provided for AP employees under the guise to be out of the fellow employee. The hackers subsequently tweeted a bogus news story by AP's accounts nevertheless two explosions choose to go in the WhiteHouse and also then-President Barack Obama was injured. This gained this kind of a substantial reaction which the stock exchange fell 150 points in just under five minutes.

Additionally in 2013, a Millionaire scam Resulted in this Huge statistics Breach of Goal. A phishing email has been provided for a H-Vac (heating, venting and airconditioning) sub contractor which has been a business partner of Target. The email included the Citadel Trojan, that allowed attackers to permeate Goal's point of sale systems and steal the info for 40 million customer credit and bank cards. That exact same year the U.S. Department of Labor was directed by means of a watering hole strike, and its particular internet sites were infected with malware by means of a vulnerability in web browser which installed a remote access Trojan termed Poison Ivy.

Back in 2015, hackers obtained access to this private AOL email Accounts of John Brennan, then a manager of the CIA. One of those hackers clarified to press outlets the way he used social engineering practices to present as a Verizon tech and ask advice regarding Brennan's report with the telecom giant. Once the hackers got Brennan's Verizon accounts information they contacted AOL and used the information to properly reply security questions to get Brennan's email accounts.

Preventing social technology

Security specialists advocate that IT departments frequently Carry-out penetration testing which employs social engineering methods. This will aid administrators learn which kinds of users pose the most risk for certain kinds of attacks, while also pinpointing which employees need additional training.

CHAPTER EIGHT
DEFENSE STRATEGIES

Defense In-depth Defined

Defense in Depth (DiD) is a way to Cyber-security in That a collection of defensive mechanics are layered as a way to safeguard valuable data and information. If one mechanism fails, then another steps up instantly to thwart an attack. This multi-layered system with deliberate redundancies escalates the security of a method altogether and addresses a number of attack vectors. Defense in Depth is often referred to as the"castle system" since it reflects the layered guards of a medieval castle. Before you may penetrate a castle you're confronted with the moat, ramparts, draw bridge ramparts, towers, battlements and so forth.

The electronic world has altered the way we live, operate and Play with. But it's really a virtual universe that's always available to strike, also as there are many possible attackers, we will need to make certain we now have the ideal security in place to stop networks and systems being endangered. Regrettably, there's not any method that could successfully force away each and every kind of strike. This really is the point where a defense at thickness architecture comes into playwith.

The Way Defense In-depth Works

A layered approach to safety could be implemented to all degrees Of all IT systems. By the only notebook obtaining the internet from the coffee shop to the fifty million user venture WAN, Defense thorough can considerably boost your profile.

No business maybe be completely shielded by one Layer of safety. Where one door might be shut, the others will probably be left open and hackers may come across these vulnerabilities quickly. But whenever you employ a collection distinct defenses together, like firewalls, malware scanners, intrusion detection systems, data security and ethics auditing solutions, you efficiently close the openings which can be made by counting upon a singular security remedy.

Components of Defense Comprehensive

Having a ever-growing landscape of safety risks to Compete with, security businesses are always developing new security services and products to safeguard systems and networks. Below Are Some of the very common security components utilized at a Defense Comprehensive plan:

Network Security Controls

The initial line of protection when procuring a system would be your Investigation of traffic. Firewalls prevent usage of and from networked networks also will block or allow traffic based on some pair of security rules. Intrusion security systems frequently work in conjunction with a firewall to recognize potential security hazards and react to them fast. In the event that you'd really like to find out more regarding network security, then see our "what's network security?" Web Page.

Anti-virus Computer Software

Anti-virus applications is Essential to Avoiding Viruses and malware. But lots of variations frequently rely heavily upon signature-based detection. When these solutions offer you strong security against malicious applications, signature-based services and products can be manipulated by intelligent cyber-criminals. Because of this, it's prudent to employ an antivirus solution which features heuristic features that scan for suspicious patterns and activity.

Analyzing Data Integrity

Every document on something gets what's referred to as a checksum. This can be really a mathematical representation of a document which shows the frequency of its usage, its own origin and that may be utilized to assess against a famous collection of viruses and other malicious code. If an incoming document is totally specific to this machine it might be pronounced as questionable. Data integrity solutions may check the origin IP address to make it from a well known and trusted source.

Behavioral Analytics

Document and community behaviors frequently provide insight while a Breach is happening or has happened. If behavioral investigation has been triggered it means the intrusion or firewall security solutions have neglected. Behavioral investigation sees the idle and may send alarms or implement automatic controls which prevent a violation from continuing further. In order for this to operate efficiently, associations will need to specify a baseline for"ordinary" behavior.

Choosing the Finest First Line of Defense

As Stated before, It's the firewall which supplies Your very first line of defense on your business's Defense comprehensive strategy. Because of this, it is logical to pick out an answer that supplies a selection of features intended to drive back an ever-evolving hazard landscape and also the shifting demands of the modern business enterprise.

Forcepoint's Nextgeneration Firewall (NGFW) defends businesses against appearing malware and different characteristics that undermine the integrity of one's data and network. Together with NGFW in place, you're able to answer events in seconds, not hours, then instantly see and determine what's going on in your system.

Why You Want Defense Indepth Cyber-security: To Maintain Your Sensitive Resources Secure

Does the cashier working a register demand accessibility to Sensitive files detailing the organization's intellectual property (IP)?) Odds would be the clear answer isn't a. But whenever there isn't any segmentation into the system, it can be too possible for somebody with this type of level of access to accomplish the sensitive systems which hold this data.

Creating defense in thickness by segmenting the system helps To make sure your company's most sensitive data will be retained dispersed (and therefore more protected). Additionally, it can help you apply a policy of freedom by keeping sensitive systems different from the people who users that lack access can utilize.

Why You Want Defense In-depth Cyber-security: To Minimize the Effect of Data Breaches

Data breaches are nearly inevitable. Eventually, there Will probably be an individual ascertained, resourceful, or blessed enough to slide beyond the perimeter defenses to begin ripping data out of the systems. Imagine having a defense in thickness cyber-security plan will not make it harder for the consumer to get whatsoever.

Rather than having carte blanche to get all at Once the moment they get beyond the perimeter, the consumer is going to need to peel each level of network security you have. This vastly raises their "break out period" (the time that it takes them to maneuver in 1 server/asset onto a system into another location), gives your system security team longer hours for you to find and cancel the strike.

When attackers can get fewer systems, they will be Inclined to undermine up to data thus reducing the seriousness and impact of almost any resulting data breaches. Yes, the data will nevertheless be endangered, but attackers becoming just non-personally-identifiable consideration information is much better than walking with sensitive info such as payment data or Social Security Numbers.

Enacting a Defense In-depth Cyber-security Policy For The Company

Building and enacting a shield at thickness Cyber-security Program For an whole company is an essential process which may need substantial time and resources. Nevertheless, the developments on your own network security will probably soon be really worth the endeavor. This installation procedure might easily be its own article, however, the basic summary is

- Audit Your Own Network. To generate effective segmentation, then you want to find out where what's in your own system. Every advantage, every portal, every sensitive document, and every program.

- Organize/Consolidate Your Sensitive Data. Perhaps not every work station in the business ought to own a backup of client/customer's PII onto it. As an alternative, sensitive data needs to really be merged on a single server/database (plus something remote backup), together with extraneous regional backups getting deleted. In this manner, if your work station is compromised, then there won't be a direct and acute data breach.

- Utilize A Few Forms of Firewalls. The margin is not the sole place to place a firewall. Businesses should utilize app-level firewalls and also end point firewalls to scrutinize traffic between nodes from the network too. This reduces the odds of an insider threat having the ability to maneuver in 1 network advantage into some other unnoticed.

- Reluctantly Tracking Firewall Configurations. Preparing a firewall isn't the end all be-all for network security. Firewalls need to be occasionally assessed and reconfigured to create certain that they are not blocking legitimate traffic or inducing network operation to dive (while maintaining their security benefits). Here, acquiring a managed security service provider (MSSP) into manage your anti-virus might be hugely helpful since it ensures effective firewall setup whilst keeping your internal IT resources to concentrate on additional targets.

Network security measures exceed simply using firewalls. Supplemental measures, like encrypting stored data, requiring employee user account to get multi-factor authentication, and using security information and event management (SIEM) methods to track cyber-security episode data may help increase system security for the own organization.

CHAPTER NINE
ATTACK STRATEGIES

In conclusion, entrepreneurs everywhere Are Searching for a Mitigation plan that restricts any possible damage whilst fulfilling their business requirements. Even in the event that you employ preventative security measures, like maintaining your site computer software uptodate, perfect cyber-security is never a guarantee, notably as hackers are persistent and utilize more complex procedures.

At Case a cyber assault breaks down through your own defenses, You need to have a plan as a way to help not just reduce response time and unplanned expenses, but in addition to safeguard your reputation. The ideal reduction strategies for cyberattacks are orderly. For that reason, a cyber-security incident response plan is now mandatory for the smaller enterprises.

Why You Want a Cyber-security Incident

Response Plan

A tactical plan outlines Just Who, what, when, where, Why, and your team will answer an attack. From the act, it keeps the answer organized.

To comprehend why using a plan for mitigating cyber Strikes is indeed essential, consider what might happen with you. To begin with, partners, customers, and investors are more very likely to shed confidence in organizations that handle strikes defectively.

For Example, when hackers uttered The info of 25 million Uber passengers and drivers at 20-16, the company failed to disclose the violation (Asis demanded for legal reasons). As an alternative, Uber paid off the hackers that a ransom, after which it the hackers resisted even longer data. The bungled response cost the company nearly $150 million in maintain resolutions -- plus a great deal longer in lost people confidence. It was a drawback for Uber, however, an identical situation could cost your little business far more.

As a Company Owner, it is your responsibility to choose the Lead to creating a cyber-security incident response program. Bear in mind, vital company stakeholders have to give their input signal and understand their own functions. You also have to think of how cyber-attacks can influence clients, providers, web programmers, along with other third parties and also can include them at the reform coverages.

A STEP BY STEP GUIDE INTO MITIGATION

The Principal aim of the incident response strategy would be to Cover every foundation. Following is a detail by detail guide to each point of a attack reply.

• Identification: on Account of this stealthy Nature of hackers, so most cyberattacks are not instantly apparent. For example, as stated by this "SiteLock 20-19 Website Security Report," 33 percent of files washed from our malware scanner were Java Script files. Java Script strikes tend to be symptomless, that explains the reason why they will have turned into a new preferred weapon of cyber-criminals.

Because of This, your event response strategy must comprise The execution of automatic safety tools to track and detect malicious actions. After the good results of cyber-attack remediation and reduction is quantified based on how fast you're able to determine an attack, then it's far better to rely on automation.

• Discovery: The Alternative is to find The character of the strike and the way it influenced the business enterprise. This usually means organizing with your internet developer or third-party collateral provider to appraise the harm. It is vital to proceed fast here in order to decrease dwell time, that is high priced. You can not educate those afflicted with the strike and soon you fully realize the range of the damage, also specifying the reach of the hazard is critical for focusing on just how to prevent it.

• Remediation and recovery: Removing All traces of this hazard demands somebody who are able to distribute every single sin in something. Unless you possess this expertise available inhouse, the cyber-security incident response program should detail who to contact.

Locate a security provider That Provides detailed Automated alternatives to get rid of traces of cyber strikes whenever possible. While this campaign is ongoing, everybody else on the team needs to really be attempting to reestablish business as usual. Planning this will continue to work helps to ensure that nothing can be overlooked and that communicating with stakeholders remains translucent.

• Inspection: when the dust has settled, Review your existing security position to find some vulnerabilities that can be tapped. This consists of communication with your team and talking what elements of this master plan has to be shifted. Becoming thorough about it review means performing a systematic test (that ought to be set out in the master plan) and will involve getting a specialist.

• Communication: Throughout this stage, Organizations should communicate the violation with their workers and execute security awareness training. This practice is intended to coach your employees on the value of using strong user names and passwords, pinpointing spam mails, and getting mindful of questionable activity which can prevent still another security violation.

• Employ: You Want to spot some other Identified weak issues with extra heights of cyber-security. That'll imply installing a stronger web application firewall, even a far improved backup solution to website and company files, and also an automated malware scanner. Implementing new security technologies usually involves additional investments, however in virtually all circumstances, prevention is less costly than yet another attack.

It is Tough to comprehend how disorderly things could eventually become later A powerful cyberattack, notably in your business, where monetary and human resources are not limited. To insure your bases, have a extensive cyber-security incident response program and make sure key stakeholders understand just how to abide by along.

CONCLUSION

Should you have Ever researched famous conflicts ever, you will recognize that no 2 will be exactly alike. Still, you will find definite plans and approaches usually utilized in conflict as they're time-proven to work.

Similarly, If an offender is seeking to hack on organization, they won't re invent the wheel till they have to: They will draw up on ordinary kinds of hacking methods which can be understood to be extremely effective, such as malware, phishing, or even cross-site scripting (XSS). Whether you are attempting to make awareness of the hottest data breach mantra from the news headlines or assessing a incident on your organization, it will help to comprehend different attack vectors a malicious celebrity may possibly attempt to cause injury. Here is an summary of a number of the very typical kinds of attacks found now.

Malware

Should you have Ever noticed an antivirus alarm popup in your monitor, or when you have wrongly clicked a malicious email attachment, and then you've experienced a close call with malware.

"Malware" Identifies several kinds of harmful applications, like viruses and ransom-ware . Once malware remains on your personal computer, it might wreak all kinds of havoc, even from taking charge of one's own machine, to tracking your activities and keystrokes, to quietly sending a variety of confidential data out of the pc or system into the attacker's home base.

Attackers Can make use of an assortment of ways to access malware in your pc, however in any point often it takes an individual to have a method to put in malware. This may consist of clicking a URL to download a document, or establishing an attachment which can appear harmless (just like a Word file or PDF attachment), but has a malware installer hidden within.

Phishing

Of Course, odds are you'll not simply open a random attachment or click a link in any email which comes your way there needs become a compelling basis that you do it. Attackers understand that, too. As soon as an attacker would like one to install malware or disclose sensitive info, they usually turn into malicious approaches, or pretending to be somebody else or another person for one to choose an activity you ordinarily would not. As they count on individual fascination and instincts, cyber-attacks might be hard to prevent.

At a Phishing attack, an individual can send you a message that seems to be from somebody that you trust, such as your boss or perhaps a company that you work with. The email will appear logical, and it'll have a urgency for this (e.g. fraudulent activity was discovered in your own accounts). From the mail, there'll undoubtedly be an attachment to either start or perhaps a hyperlink to see. Upon launching the malicious attachment, then you will hence install malware from your PC. If you follow on the connection, it can send one to some legitimate-looking site which asks that you sign into to get into an crucial document --but that the site is really a snare used to catch your credentials when you attempt to sign into.

Inorder To battle malware efforts, understanding the significance of confirming email senders and also attachments/links is vital.

SQL Injection Attack

SQL (pronounced "sequel") represents structured query language; it is really a programming language used to communicate with all databases. A number of the servers which store significant data for services and websites utilize SQL to deal with the data within their databases. A SQL injection attack expressly targets this type of host, using malicious code to have the host to disclose information it ordinarily would not. That is particularly problematic in the event the server stores confidential customer information by the site, such as credit card numbers, user names and passwords (certificate), or other personally identifiable details, that can be lucrative and tempting objectives for the attacker.

An SQL Injection attack operates by exploiting any of those famous SQL vulnerabilities that permit the SQL server to perform malicious code. By way of instance, if your SQL server is exposed to a injection attack, it might be easy for an individual to visit a site's search box and key in code which could induce your website's SQL host to ditch most its stored user names and passwords to the website.

Cross-Site Scripting (XSS)

In a SQL Injection attackan attacker moves after having a exposed internet site to a target its stored data, such as user credentials or sensitive financial data. However, when the attacker could preferably instantly aim an internet site's customers, then they can elect to get a cross-site scripting attack. Much like a SQL injection attack, this attack additionally involves putting malicious code into a site, in this event the internet site it self is never being assaulted. As an alternative, the malicious code that the attacker has recovered just rans from the consumer's browser whenever they see the assaulted internet site, also it moves after visitors right, and not the site.

Certainly one of The most typical ways an attacker may set up a cross-site scripting attack would be by injecting malicious code into an opinion or even a script which may mechanically ran. By way of instance, they can embed a URL to some malicious Java Script at a comment on the site.

Cross-site Scripting strikes may substantially harm a site's standing by setting the users' information at an increased risk with no sign that whatever malicious actually occurred. Any sensitive information that a user sends into your website -- such as with their identity, credit card info, or any other confidential data -- could be retrieved via cross site scripting minus the website owners recognizing that there is a problem at the first location.

Denial of service (DoS)

Imagine You are sitting on a one-lane country road, with cars backed up so much as the eye could see. Ordinarily this road sees over an automobile or 2, however a county fair and also a leading sporting event have stopped across precisely the exact same period, also this road could be the sole means for individuals to leave town. The trail can not deal with the huge level of traffic, so that consequently it becomes really copied that pretty much no you may render. That is essentially what goes on to a internet site in a denial of service (DoS) attack. In the event that you flood a website with more traffic than it had been constructed to take care of, you'll overload the site's server and it's going be more nigh-impossible for your own site to serve its content up for individuals that are attempting to get it.

This really is Happen for benign reasons needless to say, state should a huge news narrative breaks along with also a paper's internet site becomes bombarded with traffic from those attempting to discover more. But this sort of traffic overload is malicious, even as a attacker flooding a site by having a overwhelming quantity of traffic to essentially shut down it to users.

In certain Instances, these DoS attacks have been performed by lots of computers at precisely the exact same moment. The scenario of attack will be called a Distributed denial of service Attack (DDoS). This form of attack might be more challenging to overcome as a result of attacker arising out of numerous IP addresses across the globe simultaneously, which makes determining the foundation of the attack a lot harder for system administrators.

Session Hijacking and also Man in the Middle Attacks

When You are on the World-wide web, your computer has a great deal of small back and forth trades with servers across the globe enabling them understand that who you are and asking specific sites or solutions. But in exchange, if all goes as it should, the servers should answer your petition giving you the information you are getting. This technique, or session, happens if you're simply browsing or whenever you're logging to a website with your password and username.

The Session between the pc and the remote server is provided a exceptional session ID, which ought to stay confidential between both parties; nevertheless, an attacker may hijack the session by getting the SESSIONID and posing since the computer implementing, letting them sign into within a unsuspecting user and access bogus information online server. There are quite a few ways an attacker could use to sneak the session ID, like a cross-site scripting attack utilized to pierce session IDs.

An Attacker may also decide to ditch the session to fit themselves between the asking computer and the remote server, even pretending to become one other party inside the semester. This makes it possible for them to intercept information from both directions and is often known as a Man in the Middle attack.

Users Now have many logins and passwords to bear in mind it is tempting to reuse credentials there or here to make life somewhat simpler. Though security practices recommend you have unique passwords for most of your websites and applications, a lot of folks still reuse their passwords well known fact attackers rely upon.

Once Investors possess a selection of user names and passwords by your busted internet site or service (readily acquired on almost any range of black-market internet sites online)they understand that should they utilize these exact credentials on different internet sites there is an opportunity they will have the ability to sign into. However tempting it could be to recreate credentials for the email, banking accounts, as well as your favorite sports discussion, it is likely that a single day that the discussion will probably get hacked, even giving an attacker easy access for a bank and email accounts. In regards to credentials, number is indispensable. Password managers can be obtained and will be helpful in regards to managing the several credentials you're using.

That really is Only a choice of common attack types and methods. It's not designed to be methodical, and attackers will develop and develop new techniques as needed; nevertheless, being mindful of, and these sorts of strikes will considerably enhance your security position.

Detecting risks in your surroundings?

Boost Your assurance with incident response and detection solutions from Rapid7.

What's a Phishing Attack?

Phishing Is a societal technology security attack which tries to trick aims into divulging sensitive/valuable info. Some times known as a "phishing scam," attackers target users' login credentials, financial information (for example, credit cards or bank account), company data, and also whatever may potentially be of significance.

Enormous Organizations have been in danger of phishing attacks because of their sheer size and possibility of attackers to locate holes in their own security techniques. In case the malware attack is powerful, a member of staff falling prey into the con might put their whole company in jeopardy of prospective chaos. Businesses must assess how exposed they are to malicious attacks through penetration testing Exams and executing the findings from security awareness training programs.

Sorts of Phishing Attacks

At its Most essential definition, the expression phishing attack frequently refers to some wide attack targeted at a high numbers of users (or "goals"). This is sometimes looked at as a"quantity over quality" approach, requiring minimal prep by the attacker, with the anticipation that a couple of those goals will fall prey to it (which makes the Mini Mal up front effort attractive even although the expected profit for the attacker isn't usually all that big).

Phishing Attacks normally participate an individual with a note designed to solicit on a particular answer (usually a mouseclick) via an emotion or desire, like the following examples:

"You can get a $50 gift card into Restaurant X" (greed)
"Your Own Purchase Order was approved" (confusion)
"Your accounts will be canceled should you not sign into immediately" (concern sense of urgency)
Mail Case of a Phishing Attack:

As revealed From the info-graphic previously, you can find loads of manners which attakers can try to receive their hands in your own information with one email. But, there are frequently indicators that will help determine whether an email is valid.

Attackers Have innovated on terrorist attacks through time, making up variations that want more upfront attempt by the attacker however bring about a higher speed of sufferers or some bigger value"payout" per prey (or both!).

Spear Phishing

If a Phishing attack is customized to focus on a organization or special individual(s), it's known as spear-phishing. These strikes demand more advice accumulated in front of the time and comprise different elements such as company logos, email and website addresses of the business or alternative organizations that the provider works together with, and at times professional or individual details about a target--to be able to seem as accurate as you can. This extra attempt by the attacker has a tendency to pays with a bigger quantity of goals being scammed.

Whaling

As a Variant of this spear-phishing attack, whaling aims a business's Senior or c level executives. Whaling strikes typically take particular Responsibilities of those executive jobs under account, using focused Messaging to deceive the victim. After a whaling assault successfully dupes a Aim, the attacker's windfall might be large (e.g. high level credentials To business accounts, company secrets, etc.).

www.ingramcontent.com/pod-product-compliance
Lightning Source LLC
Chambersburg PA
CBHW061240120726
48001CB00001B/65